3-7-68

LIVING WITH COMMUNISM

CONTENTS

Living with Communism

Personal Impressions

A BACKGROUND BOOK

Anthony Sylvester, *pseud.*

DUFOUR EDITIONS

CHESTER SPRINGS

PENNSYLVANIA

FOREWORD

COMMUNISM is about economics. It has come about mainly because its fathers, Marx and Engels, as well as the man who first put it into practice in Russia, Lenin, sought an answer to the misery in which the working classes were living in the nineteenth century, and in Russia in 1917, the year of the October Revolution. An integrated theory of economic life and human history was evolved—Marxism-Leninism—which became the creed of millions. Whatever else one may say about communism, no one can deny its importance. Some thousand million people live under communist régimes. And communism continues to fire the imagination of countless men and women in the free world.

Yet quite a number of falsehoods are obvious in the doctrine of communism. Perhaps the most important of these is the contention that ordinary people in non-communist societies are bound, by virtue of some historical law, to live in worse and worse conditions while the 'exploiting minority', the capitalists and their henchmen, are getting richer and richer.

Not only is this patently untrue today, but it is doubtful if the theory was valid even during the worst periods of industrial revolution in the nineteenth century.

In the England of that time, for example, life was improving for ordinary, working-class people as opportunities of employment expanded and many new products of general consumption, such as cotton underwear, became widely available. This was a significant difference between early capitalism and Soviet industrial revolution. Capitalist industrial revolution was very largely based on consumer goods industries. The communist way of industrial development is to concentrate on heavy industry, giving very little, if any, improvement to ordinary consumers, who have been promised that at some uncertain future date the emphasis will be switched from heavy to light industries.

The communist theory of 'inevitable' pauperisation of industrial and agricultural workers received a particularly 'mighty blow' (as the communists would put it) in western Europe after the last war. Contrary to the beliefs of many communists, the downfall of Hitler did not usher in a final collapse of capitalism and 'bourgeois' democracy in Europe. There was no general economic crisis. The nations of western Europe swiftly recovered from war-time devastation and entered a period of unprecedented prosperity which has by no means ended.

Having experienced a rebuff in Europe, communist theoreticians and strategists turned to the emerging world of Africa, Latin America and Asia. 'Look', they said, 'nothing has changed. What has happened is that the problem of increasing poverty has shifted from individual nations to the entire world. The majority of mankind is now getting poorer and poorer while the capitalist-dominated West is getting richer and richer.' Marxist formula is thus supposed to be saved. Moreover, it has acquired an ominous, global ring.

Unfortunately, it is quite true that the gap between the have and the have-not nations is growing. But this has nothing to do with Marxist analysis. (Although it *is* true that communist theories and strategies have led to a sharper awareness among the privileged people of affluent nations of the menace to themselves which the problems of world poverty, malnutrition and backwardness pose.)

But it has nothing to do with Marxism, because Marxism tries to explain history as a battle of classes whereby one class exploits another until the underdogs get the upper hand. It is not true to say that the Western nations have become rich because they exploited Africans, Asians and Latin Americans—not, at least, as a generalisation. It is true that many colonial peoples had a rough deal in the past and it is now almost universally agreed among governments and peoples in the West that peoples everywhere should have the right to govern themselves. The era of colonialism in the classical sense is, for all practical purposes, over and dead.

8

Yet it is not widely realised that few colonies had actually been a source of net profit to the metropolitan country—not within the last hundred years or so, at any rate. Indeed, colonies were by no means solely or even mainly acquired for economic reasons, such as the pursuit of markets. They were acquired chiefly to satisfy a somewhate primitive, immature hankering after power and influence. Incidentally, the only large empire that has not been liquidated recently is that of Russia.

Most of the trade that the advanced Western nations were conducting at the height of the colonial empires in the second half of the nineteenth and the beginning of the twentieth centuries was among themselves, not with the colonial world of coloured races. Western nations became wealthy not because they had exploited the poor masses of Africa, Asia and Latin America, or the riches of these continents, but because of their own natural resources, skills and the will to get rich. When Britain gave up her empire, which was the greatest the world had ever seen, this was not followed by an economic collapse of the mother country, as it should have been logically, according to communist theories. On the contrary, people in Britain live now better than they have ever done in the past. Britain's exports are now greater than ever before, although the proportion of shipments going to former colonies and dominions has decreased.

This is not to say that the West has no responsibility for the well-being of the less privileged populations. Indeed it owes it to itself and its children that galling inequalities in the world should be removed and genuine partnership established between the rich and those who are trying to become so. Far from being in conflict with each other, the two halves—the northern and southern halves of the world —have every interest in working together. But this only proves the fallacy and irrelevance of communist theories on the subject.

This book is not about communist theory and its incompatibility with the everyday facts of life. I am satisfied that learned authors have established this beyond reasonable doubt. Neither do I wish to demonstrate the superiority of the Western way of life over that in the communist orbit, although some implications of what I am saying may be so interpreted.

The buoyant prosperity of the West and the frustrations and miseries of life in the East are indeed obvious to any open-minded traveller. But there are many other reasons, apart from the difference in social and economic systems, which must be taken into account when comparing, say, the standard of living in the USA with that in the Soviet Union. Many communist countries have started from scratch. They have had hundreds of years of backwardness and neglect behind them. They have been devastated by wars and revolutions (sometimes, of course, due to communists themselves).

To say that the superiority of the Western way of life is proved by the fact an American (or Western German) workman can now easily afford to buy himself a car while a Russian cannot, is silly and vulgar. It is of little interest to the rest of the world, anyway. Cars are beyond the reach of most people in the world.

Finally, what I am saying in this little book is not meant to be unfriendly to communists, especially those in whose countries I have been. In many socialist countries I have been received well; in some very well indeed. In Cuba particularly I was treated as an honoured guest and given, during a visit which lasted a month, every facility by the government to see what they thought was worth seeing. And I was in no way prevented from seeing more.

I had some unpleasant experiences in Russia, where inquisitive travellers are not yet fully accepted. But I can now fully endorse the view that contacts have become very much easier with the 'other half' and that people in those countries, if not always keen on talking, are none the less almost invariably hospitable, friendly and interested in a stranger coming from the West, especially when knowing their languages sufficiently to be able to converse.

This book is largely about those people, about what they

told me and what I saw of their life. In this sense it is meant as a modest contribution to the dialogue that has now so hopefully been opened between West and East. But for such dialogue to be fruitful frankness is essential on both sides.

*   *   *

I was myself born in a country which later became communist: Yugoslavia. I lived through the tribulations and savage conflicts that led to the triumph of the Tito partisans —a baffled spectator most of the time, rather than a fighter. I appreciated the significance and attraction of the new creed and had many friends who devoted their lives to it.

There is a great deal to be said, even from a strictly intellectual point of view, for having been committed to a belief, fighting for its sake and sharing in its triumph—and then becoming disillusioned. Our knowledge and understanding of communism would be lacking but for those who have absconded to the West and written of their experience.

I have personally never been really attracted or convinced by communist arguments. This may sometimes put me at a disadvantage when trying to understand those who are committed to a mass movement designed to bring about a radical improvement in human existence. But then again, I think I am not very different in this respect from most people, this side or that of the Iron Curtain. If anything, my travels on the other side have convinced me that ordinary people are very much alike everywhere in the world. Basically, they want to live in peace and reasonable comfort, to work for themselves and their families before toiling for anyone else. They wish to be free from undue compulsion and to have some control over those who rule them. They want to enjoy their pleasures and pursuits, by and large innocent. In this sense, communist ambitions to create a new type of human being have patently failed, for better or for worse. The fact that such an important communist as (in his time) Nikita Khrushchev more or less admitted this and proclaimed what became widely known as 'goulash' communism makes things easier. We know what we are talking about.

I

The Triumphant Heretic

Yugoslavia

'WE SHALL ALSO SHOOT AT GOD', Darko said as we walked, immersed in our discussion. This was in Ljubljana, the place of our birth. We were schoolmates and seventeen. The year was 1938. Darko had large, limpid brown eyes, a high forehead from which his hair was combed back. He wore plusfours trousers, then very popular with young men.

He told me he was taking part in secret activities in which boys and girls of our age were being trained to handle rifles and hand grenades. 'A world war is bound to break out soon', he said, 'and then it will be time for the people, the *real* people, to take their fate in their own hands.'

He was a communist. He knew all the answers. I remember how I envied the self-confidence which the Marxist books—French translations of the works of Lenin and Stalin and others, smuggled into Yugoslavia—had given him. I could only mumble clichés, about the good old traditions that should be preserved, about Yugoslavia being a country of peasants and churchgoers. 'Communism, even if right, is not practicable in our conditions,' I said, not knowing how better to counter his sharp arguments.

I recall vividly the conversations I had with Darko and his belief that our world could be changed overnight into something much better and brighter. He showed me an article in a monthly magazine to which a leading Slovene communist, Edvard Kardelj, the future theoretician and chief strategist of Tito's Yugoslavia, also contributed. In that article someone had written that the victory of the working class in Yugoslavia would be followed by a complete transformation of the countryside. Villages, with their thatched roofs and muddy lanes would be turned into hygienic settlements of quadrangular, clean houses with large windows. Somehow I disliked the vision. . . .

But when I drove, twenty-seven years later, from Ljubljana to Belgrade, I remembered that article as I looked at large women in black kerchiefs working in the fields as they had done through centuries, and at the villages which were just as I remembered them from my youth, except that more of the thatched roofs seemed to be in need of repair.

Darko was a commissar when the war came. He was caught by 'village guards' when a former schoolmate recognised him. He was shot dead, and his body was quartered by angry peasants.

Darko's father was a railway worker; mine was a senior civil servant of the old Austrian school. Darko grew up in a rickety hut; I lived in a comfortable flat with dark-green curtains, large sofas and armchairs, and photographs of stout, moustached men in Austrian uniforms staring from the walls.

I always thought that a good deal could be said in favour of the defunct monarchy, its sense of form, tolerance and humanity, its efficient and impartial government which, taking the country as a whole, compared well with what was to follow the rule of the Habsburgs. It was perhaps a tragedy that many of the men who mattered most in the Empire and Kingdom seemed to have lost confidence in themselves and instead began to stake their fortunes on the German and Hungarian nationalism.

My favourable views of life under the double-headed black eagle, as I learned about it from my parents and relatives, did not make me popular with my friends. Yet, for that matter, Darko too was far from being typical of the young men of his age in his home town. I knew sons and daughters of rich men, merchants and industrialists, who became fanatical communists. I also knew many young people of working class or poor peasant families who passionately hated all that communism stood for.

Communism and anti-communism certainly did not run along class lines in Yugoslavia to anything like the extent they did in Russia at the time of the October Revolution.

But it was true that a talented young man without money or good connections could achieve little in old Yugoslavia unless he had a university degree or was a genius of some sort. It was also true that there were very many impecunious graduates about with nothing much to do—not only law graduates but also scientists and engineers.

There can be little doubt that among the frustrated young intelligentsia a fertile ground for communism was to be found. Yet many of these men and women sincerely believed that the coming revolution was to usher in a new world of unprecedented prosperity for the people at large, was to do away with backwardness and other evils of the old 'bourgeois' societies as well as bring about an economic and political assertion of the Yugoslav nation as such.

Nationalism was inextricably wedded to communism in the minds of these young radicals. But this was a fairly recent development. It could be traced back to 1937 when Josip Broz, later known as Tito, took command of the Party, gathered around him a bunch of exceptionally gifted younger men, and pinned to his mast the banner of brotherhood of all Yugoslav peoples—at a time when much of Yugoslav politics was made up of quarrels between nationalities, especially between the Serbs and the Croats.

The Party, of course, stood for Soviet Russia, a distant, controversial, yet to many a vaguely attractive country, peopled by fellow-Slavs. Russia suddenly became exceedingly significant in view of the rise and claims of Nazi Germany. Somehow, the communists succeeded in convincing many, at any rate in Slovenia, that national ambitions, cruelly thwarted after the First World War, could only be fulfilled if advanced by a party standing for the working class, because the majority of the population in the chief target areas of Slovene nationalism—in the Slovene littoral held by Italy and in Carinthia (Austria)—were 'proletarians' among whom were known to be many communist and other left-wing supporters, especially among the Italians in Trieste.

True, the Communist Party in pre-war Yugoslavia was still very small numerically. There were only some 13,000 organised members in a nation of about 15 million. Even together with their supporters the communists were vastly inferior in numbers to those who were violently opposed to them: the traditional Serbian monarchists backed by the Army, the Croatian nationalists, the Slovene Catholic Party and several others of lesser significance. It would have been quite inconceivable for the communists to win at a free general election, or even to receive a substantial vote.

The transformation of this small, hounded Communist Party into a mass movement which had won the civil war in Yugoslavia and persuaded most of the world that it was the true and unchallenged representative of the people it claimed to rule is one of those puzzling phenomena of human history; it certainly cannot be explained in Marxist terms.

Of course Marxism was not entirely irrelevant. It is quite true that the communist movement gave the opportunity and self-confidence to many young people of working-class origin and little formal schooling to rise to positions of command and influence during the war. They might have risen with the help of other parties and movements, but that would have been less likely.

One great advantage which the communists possessed at the very beginning of their bid for power in 1941, when the 'old order' collapsed ignominiously under the impact of German tanks and Stuka aircraft, was that of initiative. The great majority of the Yugoslav people obviously wanted the Germans to leave and the Allies to win the war. This also applied to nearly all pre-war political parties and leaders. But these men were largely putting their faith in victorious outsiders. They did little, or not enough, to help the Allied cause and assert themselves.

But it is very difficult to generalise about Yugoslavia, a country of many nationalities, traditions and faiths. It would be quite untrue to claim that the Yugoslav nation stood united in its dislike of the invader. Some of those who believed themselves to have been wronged in the old, monarchistic Yugoslavia—Croatian extremists, pro-Bulgarian Macedonians, large sections of the Albanian and Hungarian minorities and indeed the Yugoslav Germans—hailed the Nazi victories as a new dawn for their own ambitions. The Ustashi fascist régime in Croatia, headed by Ante Pavelich, was much discredited subsequently, but I remember distinctly that very many in Croatia of 1941 considered it a welcome event. I remember the abuses which were hurled at us young Slovene volunteers of the Yugoslav Army as we marched through Croatian villages. This was a time when many 'reasonable' men believed that Adolf Hitler would win the war, or at any rate would not be defeated.

It is against this background of confusion—ignominious debacle for some and borrowed triumph for others—that the impact made by the communists must be understood. The world one knew seemed to have collapsed and vanished beyond redemption. Dark forces of unprecedented violence and brutality took over the scene. Now anything was possible.

'I never thought the Germans would do that,' an old friend of mine, himself of Germanic extraction, said to me as we stood in a crowd of thousands, in silent protest, in Italian-occupied Ljubljana. It was only a month or so after the German invasion. Train after train of sealed trucks passed by, escorted by shouting, steel-helmeted Germans. Slovenes were being deported from their ancestral homes to the south, to Serbia. Many other and far worse brutalities were committed by the German invaders. But this event will always stick in mind. My German friend had tears in his eyes. He realised that for a very long time now the Germans, good or bad, would be hated in Slovenia.

The scene was set for a communist revolution. Immediately the communists began to gather their forces. It is true that they were not actually first to resist the German invaders. A former colonel of the Yugoslav Army, a left-wing idealist, but basically a loyal royalist Serb, Drazha Mikhailovich, originally stole the limelight as a hero of the Yugoslav mountains. He drew much of his strength initially from the Serbian element which fled into the woods for fear of vengeance-seeking Croatian fascists. A valiant man and a good patriot himself, Mikhailovich put his finger on the crux of the matter when he declared at his trial in Belgrade, in 1946 '... the whirlwind of the world carried me and my work away.' He was soon after executed by the triumphant communists.

* * *

Apart from knowing exactly what they wanted, the Yugoslav communists entered the battle arena with a whole gamut of new tricks and expertise. Not only did they come with a promising political and social philosophy, they also knew how to combine military action with political education. This was new in Yugoslavia, where the old division between soldier and politician was still widely accepted. They also possessed superior military knowledge as many of their men had just returned from years of fighting in the Spanish Civil War. They knew, above all, how little an aeroplane could really do in a wooded, mountainous country.

The communists were also completely devoid of any scruples of 'bourgeois' morality. This was an important asset, although it could sometimes be a double-edged weapon. I remember the horror and disgust many people felt when the body of a widely respected man, a priest and university teacher, was found one morning, lying in the street in Ljubljana riddled by bullets fired by a communist attacker. This was only one of a vast number of actions by which the communists rid themselves of their political opponents and rivals.

I remember when in 1942 I took part in guerrilla fighting with Partisans and was dumbfounded by the methods which they employed. We used to occupy villages, five or six of us, and then retreat swiftly into the mountains when hundreds of Italians, or Germans, drove us away. The village was captured, the houses burned down by the invaders, some of the peasants shot on the spot and others deported with their families. 'This helps people to develop a revolutionary awareness,' the commander of our unit explained when I questioned the wisdom of our actions.

One day in the summer of 1942 a detachment of Partisan guerrillas in our area attacked a train. After considerable shooting and a number of casualties on both sides it transpired that this was a transport of students and other young people who had been rounded up indiscriminately by the panicking Italians in Ljubljana and dispatched to a concentration camp. The Partisans liberated three hundred men from the train. The following morning, a senior communist official arrived in the forest glade where the crowd of the new arrivals had assembled.

'No one is forced to join us,' he said in a persuasive tone. 'The choice is yours. You can come and fight with us, or else go back to your homes. We shall provide escort to the nearest Italian post.' I was worried. 'But surely,' I said to a seasoned Partisan, 'you cannot let these men go home just like that. They have seen us and will tell the Italians we're fighting in the mountains. Our families will suffer.' The Partisan gave me a wry grin. 'This is only our way of separating the chaff from the grain. Anyone really insisting on going home will be shot.'

Initially, well over half the boys in the glade opted for a return to the Italians. But gradually more and more developed second thoughts. Some had friends among the Partisans, who gave them a clue. Not more than eleven were left when darkness fell and the selection was completed. They were stripped of their clothes, escorted to the interior of the forest and shot dead.

I knew then that something new and unprecedented was happening to my people. To be sure, violence was no stranger to the Yugoslav political scene. But the communists brought in a new dimension, as it were. Death became a normal tool of planned political warfare, and it was quite cold-bloodedly employed. Not only direct opponents were struck down without mercy but also those who lacked the conviction of going the whole way with the Liberation Front.

Yet such methods served the communists by instilling terror into the hearts of the people. The communists went ahead relentlessly. By 1943 it was clear to the British and the Americans that Tito's Partisans—communist or not—were attacking and killing Germans more effectively than anybody else in Yugoslavia, and that was what mattered to the Allies.

* * *

'The British will never allow the communists to take over. You ought to study the history of the Balkans,' Branko said to me in Ljubljana about six months before the end of the war. Branko wore a nice new uniform of the 'Home Guard' forces set up under German auspices. Only recently Branko and his men had had to swear their allegiance to Hitler.

When the war ended Branko and over 11,000 other members of the Slovene 'Home Guard' Army were handed back to Tito by the British, from Austria where they had retreated, on the basis of a previous agreement with Yugoslav authorities. Back in Yugoslavia they were led in groups of ten or twenty to the mouths of caves and shot in the neck. Branko and nearly all the others perished in this way.

Mass extraditions were later stopped when the news reached Allied headquarters of what was going on in Yugoslavia. Many years later, I met a man in Britain who had actually escaped from one of those caves. The communist executioners believed he was dead as he fell unconscious some 30 feet down. But he was only slightly wounded. He worked his way up, through the mass of bleeding corpses, into the silent night above. He crawled past a sentry and hid in a village. He is now a prosperous businessman in Wales. Incidentally, he married a girl in Britain whose entire family was 'liquidated' by the Partisans during the war. She herself was aged 14 at the time and hid herself under the body of her father. She too received a bullet, but remained silent and managed to pass for dead.

Out of every thousand Yugoslavs more than one hundred died an unnatural death in the last war. The vast majority of them were not victims of the German or other invaders. They fell at the hands of their own countrymen.

The politically relevant fact, however, was that by 1944 the communist Partisans appeared as the only coherent force fighting the Germans. All their opponents at home had been driven into the humiliating position of German collaborators. or else were tolerated by the invaders as a lesser evil. I remember that spring of 1945, in Ljubljana, when various anti-communist forces were retreating under the cover of the German Army. The most grotesque of these men were soldiers sporting extremely long beards. They were Mikhailovich's men. They had pledged to stay in the woods and not to shave until the King returned to the liberated country.

When the war was over Tito's Partisans were complete masters of the country. Even the Russians, who had a major share in liberating Belgrade and now occupied a stretch of northern Yugoslavia, were there solely by agreement with the Yugoslav Government, as allies.

To many this seemed the fulfilment of an age-old dream. Numerous poets and writers hailed the triumphant communists as liberators. This was the time when the downtrodden South Slav nations were vindicated by the triumph of armed forces and were joined in victory by their brothers, the Russians.

'All we want now is to be incorporated into the USSR. This cannot long be delayed,' a well-known communist told me soon after the war. This was the prevailing mood among the communists and their supporters in Yugoslavia. Russia was the power which had just crushed Hitler's Germany, the most deadly enemy the Slavs had ever faced. And

Russia was now helping the Yugoslavs to fulfil their historic ambitions, above all to gain Trieste in the north-west, Carinthia in the north and Salonica in the south.

'Tito-Stalin' was the ubiquitous slogan on walls and it was chanted by multitudes at public gatherings. The busts of the two leaders were prominently displayed in streets, offices, taverns and even in the overcrowded jails. '*Trst je Naš*'—'Trieste is Ours'—was another prominent slogan. And I remember watching Greek 'freedom fighters' marching through the streets of Ljubljana waving their banners. Ironically, a less revolutionary and pro-Russian Yugoslav government would no doubt have had a far better chance of seeing the fulfilment of national ambitions. The western Allies called a halt to further expansion of Yugoslavia. A substantial, mainly Slav-populated part was ceded to Yugoslavia by Italy, but Trieste remained beyond reach, and so did Carinthia and Salonica.

What was not known to me then was that the Russians too looked upon Yugoslavia with feelings of growing mistrust and animosity. When the break finally occurred, in June 1948, this came as a complete surprise to most of the world, including Yugoslavia. We now know that there had been friction and resentment already during the war when the Russians failed to give any effective assistance to Yugoslav partisans, whose leader, Marshal Tito, had at one point to be rescued by the British. There was more friction after the war when Russian soldiery raped and looted in Yugoslavia as if they had been occupying an enemy territory.

But most important was the complete divergence of views between Stalin and the Belgrade leaders on the future role of Yugoslavia, economic and political. Past masters of *realpolitik* in other ways, the Yugoslav communist leaders still had a wholly romantic notion about the Soviet Union and its leader. Throughout the bitter fighting against incredible odds the Yugoslav communists were sustained by their faith in the Soviet Union. The man who later probably did more than anyone to debunk the myth of the USSR and indeed of communism, Milovan Djilas, the celebrated author of *The New Class*, wrote a poem in the war in which he compared Stalin to the sun. The song we Partisans were most often made to sing, when marching through villages or sitting around camp fires in 1942, said:

> Somewhere there is a land
> Where freedom rules,
> Where worker and peasant
> are lords.

The land, of course, was Russia. The Yugoslav communists, as Milovan Djilas, then one of the leaders in Belgrade but now serving a prison sentence for his writings, has explained, were genuinely shocked to find the men in the Kremlin to be as calculating, cold-blooded 'imperialists' as the world had ever known.

The shock experienced by Yugoslav leaders was not the first or the last disappointment of various communists with Moscow. But now, for the first time, two communist countries, sovereign and independent, were at loggerheads. The story has been often told, and now, looking back on the Stalin-Tito conflict of 1948–53, events appear less sensational than they did at the time yet much was learned then of Soviet tactics, and the lesson has not lost a great deal of its original significance.

To be sure, Stalin was not prepared to engage in any new international adventure with Tito's Yugoslavia. From the start he looked on the Marshal, the successful, good-looking, popular new man in the Balkans, with suspicion mixed with envy. Used to regard foreign communists with complete contempt and to employ them as mere pawns in his schemes, he was now faced with a new situation: a communist who refused to toe the line, and yet remained in power.

What Stalin did was not unrational, from his own point of view. Tito was ostracised, declared a traitor and 'running dog' of Wall Street capitalists, and anyone found in favour of him in the Soviet orbit was promptly eliminated. As far as the communist world was concerned, Tito was isolated. He was driven into the fold of the Western powers, who generously supported him, enabling him and Yugoslavia to survive. The USA, Britain and France supplied Yugoslavia with free aid and credits worth 481 million dollars between 1949 and the end of 1954.

★   ★   ★

In the eyes of the world the Tito-Stalin conflict looked like a contest between David and Goliath. But then Goliath began to look foolish. Stalin, the bully, said he would turn his little finger and there would be no more Tito. Yet the Marshal survived and was gaining in prestige, not only in the West but in the Soviet orbit too. Tito began to symbolise resistance to Soviet great-power imperialism and to all that was worst in communism.

The consequences of this rebellion went much farther than the Yugoslav communists had ever envisaged. In eastern Europe the Yugoslav example certainly helped to unleash the spirits which Russia was unable to control— even with the *help* of President Tito after Moscow and Belgrade patched up their quarrel in 1955. The treatment of Yugoslavia at the hands of Russia before the break and after and the subsequent disillusionment of the Yugoslav leaders remained of major topical significance even when the Belgrade leaders began to play down their former disagreements with Moscow. Last, but not least, Yugoslavia's economic changes and reforms revealed the dilemma faced by a communist Government which is trying to do away with the worst aspects of Soviet-type economy.

When the war ended the Yugoslav communists seemed confident that the country could now be swiftly transformed into an advanced industrial nation from one in which farming provided the living for some three-quarters of the population. First among the post-war communist régimes in eastern Europe, the Yugoslavs launched a five-year plan of economic development in 1947. Much of this development was to be based on supplies of industrial equipment provided by the rest of the communist world, especially the Soviet Union. Under an agreement signed in summer 1947, the Soviet government pledged itself to supply Yugoslavia with factory plant and other capital goods worth 135 million dollars. According to a Yugoslav White Book, the Soviet bloc as a whole promised a total of 375 million dollars worth of machinery and other goods in this period, but when a total blockade of Yugoslavia was instituted by the Soviet bloc countries in 1949 only 6·3 per cent of the goods had been received. Russia herself fulfilled less than 1 per cent of her pledges. The damage caused by the communist blockade of Yugoslavia was later estimated at 600 million dollars.

By 1947 over half of Yugoslavia's trade was with the Soviet bloc. Valuable commodities such as copper, zinc and lead, which could then have been sold with much greater profit on world markets, were sent to the Soviet Union and other communist countries, often in exchange for third-rate industrial goods. Yugoslav civil aviation and inland shipping were placed under Soviet-dominated mixed companies.

Dr Vladimir Dedijer, then an influential friend of Tito, explained later in a biography of the Marshal: 'the fundamental cause of the conflict [with the USSR] was an attempt by the Soviet Government to exploit our country economically'. The Soviet Union, he said, attempted to seal off eastern Europe economically in order to gain absolute mastery over the economic life of those countries. Analysing Soviet-Yugoslav economic relations before the break in 1948, Dedijer said: 'they clearly indicated that the Soviet Union intended to subjugate Yugoslavia economically, to prevent Yugoslavia's industrialisation and to delay further socialist development of our country'.

It is significant that during a visit to Bucharest in 1965 I found the Rumanians making similar comments to me about their much more recent experience with the USSR.

For Yugoslavia there were further disappointments in store even after the original quarrel had been patched up and Khrushchev's wooing of Yugoslavia was accompanied by promises of large-scale economic aid. In the wake of the reconciliation between Belgrade and Moscow, in 1955, important agreements were signed to provide Yugoslavia with industrial plant. In 1956, the total value of these agreements with the Soviet Union and other communist countries amounted to 464 million dollars. But when relations cooled again as Yugoslavia and 'revisionism' were blamed for the upheavals in the Soviet bloc (including the Hungarian uprising in the autumn of 1956) and Yugoslav communists persisted in their pursuit of independent national policies and ideology, most of these pledges were broken by 1958.

But now Yugoslavia had developed lively trade and economic relations with the West, and exchanges with the rest of the communist world never went up beyond some 30 per cent of Yugoslavia's total trade. This was still the case in the early sixties when political and ideological relations between Belgrade and Moscow became very intimate again. Yugoslavia has become an associate member of the Soviet Bloc economic organisation, the CMEA, or COMECON. But when I asked a Yugoslav economist in 1964 whether this meant that Yugoslavia would now participate to a much greater extent in the schemes of this organisation in eastern Europe and her trade would again be predominantly with the East he denied this emphatically. 'We have no great changes in mind,' he said. 'A certain amount of trade with Russia and the rest of the socialist world is useful to us. But we shall never want to be really dependent on them again.'

*   *   *

Even more far-reaching was the disappointment in Yugoslavia with the Soviet-type economic system. This too was originally believed by the communists to be the answer to all contemporary economic problems. After seizing power

25

the communists in Yugoslavia hastened to copy as closely as possible the centrally planned and administered economy which is practised in the Soviet Union. It was significant that even for some time after the break with Stalin's Russia the Yugoslavs continued to apply Stalinist economic principles at home. But this, coupled of course with the difficulties arising from economic blockade, led to a disastrous economic situation by the end of 1950. An agonising reappraisal began which led to a series of reforms and changes, and by the end of 1951 much of the old system was discarded, including the very idea of normative planning and economy administered by directives from the centre. The disappointment with this system—which is still largely in use in other communist countries—was profound.

A leading Yugoslav economist, Professor Rudolf Bičanić, said at a seminar in Tokyo in 1957: 'To those who lived under a system of centralised, bureaucratic, normative planning, its expense in human and economic terms, and the damage which it can do to all levels of the economy is obvious.... The balancing of supplies and demand in a centrally planned economy occurs in offices on the level of the central State planning authorities, where a few people, unaware of the real effects of their authoritarian plans become the supreme judges of the destinies of all producers and consumers through their bureaucratic machine. From this source of authority plans lead further down to smaller bodies, splitting unrealistic averages into still smaller averages, according to norms born in offices, which, when they reach the enterprise level, have little resemblance to the conditions of real life.'

Such views were echoed years later by reformers in eastern Europe and Russia, and Yugoslavia became a Mecca for all those in other communist countries who were looking for a way out of the impasse into which the Stalinist system had led them.

Of all the reforms which were introduced in Yugoslavia after the break with Stalinism that of 'workers' self-govern-

26

ment', decreed in 1950, has been the most widely publicised and closely associated with 'Titoism'—but is in truth one of the least significant or relevant. In theory, management of Yugoslav industrial and other enterprises and institutions was handed over to the employees and their elected organisations. On paper, the authority of the 'workers' council' is great and has been growing right to the present day. Even the director of the enterprise is now officially appointed, or dismissed, only by the 'workers' council'. These councils are elected by the employees for periods of two years on the basis of candidate lists which are normally submitted by the trade union organisation. Even individual departments of an enterprise now have their own 'workers' councils', responsible for the affairs of the particular unit. Councils in their turn appoint Management Boards which are entrusted with the day-to-day running of the enterprise, while the workers' council retains the ultimate authority in such important matters as the production plan, investment outlays and divisions of profits, remuneration of the employees (including that of the director himself), and recruitment and dismissal of labour. In theory, the role of the director has been limited to his being the representative of the enterprise in dealing with the outside world and a guardian of legality.

In practice, very strict limits are set to industrial democracy in Yugoslavia. For one thing, the general level of education among industrial workers in Yugoslavia is still very low. Many of these workers are half-peasants who have little understanding of industrial life. Usually these workers accept without question what the management tell them. Outside authorities, notably the *komuna* or local authority, retain important powers of intervention in case the national interest is at stake.

Moreover, the national interest is protected by a large number of frequently changing laws and regulations. The 'workers' council' is obliged to run the enterprise as a 'good manager', which entails a duty to divide the profits (if any) which are left after various deductions have been

27

made for the benefit of outside authorities in such a way that a reasonable share is channelled for reinvestment and reserves and the rest is used for the benefit of the employees in the form of housing and amenities and cash. In deciding on the way the profits are shared the 'workers' council' is governed by the charter of the enterprise which has been adopted by the employees, but it must be approved by outside authorities. By and large, the division of profits, notably the part that is ploughed back, must follow the practice of the enterprise in recent years and the custom of other enterprises in the area. Something like 30 per cent of the Yugoslav national income is invested annually. As regards the remuneration of the employees this must be strictly in line with productivity and the actual performance of the workers.

Finally, in a country whose entire life is dominated by the Communist Party (or League of Communists) which retains an absolute monopoly of power and ultimate responsibility for all political and economic decisions, workers' democracy is bound to be correspondingly curtailed. The trade union organisation in every enterprise is itself an important watchdog of the public interest as interpreted by the Party. It is only when communists themselves are disunited that violent arguments sometimes take place in Yugoslav enterprises over important issues. But this is the exception rather than the rule.

The men who still matter most in every enterprise are its director and one or two of his close assistants. In nearly all cases of industrial enterprises directors are themselves members of the Party and subject to its internal discipline. None the less, a director of a Yugoslav enterprise will do well not to antagonise his 'workers' council' unnecessarily, and will above all try to be on good terms with the outside authorities, particularly his *komuna*. 'Workers' councils' do, however, exercise significant powers in some fields, notably in labour relations and in less important matters affecting the workers directly, such as tea-breaks or canteen facilities.

More significant is the fact that enterprises as such, run

as they are largely by their directors, have been given very wide powers and they can be found competing with each other for supplies and labour as well as markets, in very much a capitalist fashion. At least equally important has been the co-operation which Yugoslavia and her industrial enterprises achieved with capitalist companies in the West. Between 1954 and 1964 Yugoslavia concluded 341 licensing contracts with foreign agencies, all but 9 per cent of them with Western companies.

*   *   *

When I returned to Yugoslavia in 1961, after an absence of many years, as a correspondent of a Western radio organisation, the country looked very different from what it was when I left at the time of Stalinism. The impression was particularly marked as I had just returned from an extended visit to the rest of the European communist world, including the Soviet Union.

Shops in Yugoslavia were well stocked with all manner of consumer goods, many approaching Western quality. Food was in plentiful supply. Slovenia looked outwardly almost like neighbouring Italy and Austria. There was much industrial activity and new, large buildings, including blocks of flats, were changing the skyline of towns. There were far more private cars on the roads, especially small Fiats made under licence in Yugoslavia, than in other communist countries.

There was a general atmosphere of euphoria and not only directors of enterprises but men of independent professions, such as lawyers and doctors, as well as artisans, seemed to be doing well. 'It's almost like before the war,' a lawyer friend of mine said. 'Our enterprises litigate in the courts, just as private companies did in the past.'

The outward appearance of affluence in certain towns and regions could be misleading when one tried to assess the situation in the country as a whole. Many people were evidently still very poor. The average income of a Yugoslav industrial worker was something like a quarter of that of his counterpart in Western Europe—a generalisation which is still broadly true today. But the standard of living of a Yugoslav worker was undoubtedly higher than that of his counterpart in the Soviet Union, or for that matter in Poland. Rationing was now by the purse only, and the average consumer was certainly coming into his, or her, own again.

Above all I was impressed by the modesty and open-mindedness of the Yugoslav communists. These now appeared as friendly, civilised men wearing good clothes, anxious to please and keen to learn from what they had been seeing in the West. Some of the more fanatical element had been eliminated from influence during the preceding witch-hunt of Cominform sympathisers. Many people had joined the Party out of opportunism but remained basically 'bourgeois' in their views and attitudes.

Many problems remained unsolved, especially that of underdevelopment in the more backward regions in the south of Yugoslavia. These problems were further exacerbated by a very rapid increase of population. But when I visited some of these southern regions, notably Macedonia, I could see that a great number of ultra-modern factories, hydro-electric projects and other industrial establishments had sprung up like mushrooms—against a background that had changed little since the Middle Ages.

When my plane landed at Ohrid, on the Albanian border, turbaned shepherds could be seen with their flocks on the fringes of the small, bumpy airfield. Young girls in colourful pantaloons turned away their faces as one looked at them. The veils had been abolished by law, yet old traditions and superstitions died hard. In villages in the neighbourhood of Ohrid lived side by side in precarious co-existence a multitude of races and religions: Macedonians, Albanians, Serbs, Turks, Gipsies, Vlachs—people of Greek Orthodox, Roman Catholic and Muslim faiths. Men and women of each group wore distinctive garments and head-gear. Each community was still a world in itself, looking on outsiders with suspicion and even hostility. Only recently many of these nationalities and faiths were at each other's throats. The communists finally imposed their stern, unpopular rule. But the old sentiments and loyalties still clearly ran deep.

New industries were now changing the lives of many of these people by offering them full-time or part-time employment in factories. But those who could not avail themselves of these fresh opportunities lived a primitive life, often on the verge of starvation and destitution.

I went with a friend around villages near Skopje, the capital of Macedonia. We stopped in front of a cottage. A barefooted, middle-aged man wearing off-white pants and a white skull-cap (the mark of an Albanian) gave us a friendly, toothless smile and showed us in.

'Taxes are too high' was the first comment he made after I had asked him how he was getting on. He owned four acres of land, a fairly typical holding in the area. He said he managed to keep hunger away from his door, somehow, for himself, his wife and two children. But there was little left over. Still, he was pleased that the authorities left him in peace and no longer forced him to join a collective.

We entered his house, a dilapidated wooden structure. There were three head of cattle on the ground floor. 'They keep the house warm in winter,' he explained. The family lived on the upper floor, in two rooms. What struck me was that there was no furniture whatsoever in either of the rooms. Placed against the wall was a straw mat which the family used at night to sleep on.

Pumping investment resources into backward regions is one way of lifting the unprivileged from their poverty and neglect. But such resources must be paid for by others, that is by the more advanced republics, notably Slovenia and Croatia. This now provides one of the main topics of argument in Yugoslavia, as the old inter-racial animosities have been reappearing under a Marxist-Leninist guise.

But economically the most relevant aspect of the matter is

31

that investments in less developed regions are often far less productive than they would have been if made in the north and north-west of the country. Productivity in less developed regions of Yugoslavia is very low, even when quite modern machinery is used. The point that soon was bound to be raised was: can the country afford costly projects in backward regions at a time when old-established factories in areas of high labour productivity and good reserves of skill are starved of modern equipment? The plain answer is it can't. But it was not only a matter of priorities, of trying to raise the level of one section of the population at the expense of another. More crucial was the fact, increasingly admitted and openly discussed in the Yugoslav press, that much of the newly established industrial enterprise was really not paying its way. It had to be generously subsidised by the nation.

Meanwhile lip service continued to be paid to economic laws of profitability and the survival of the fittest. The Titoist philosophy came to be described as a marriage between capitalism and communism. But in reality the basic principle of capitalism—that industrial enterprise should be profitable—was very often not observed.

When I was in Yugoslavia again in 1964 an economist said to me, 'The trouble with us is that we have not carried out our principles of socialist market economy and profitability of enterprises at all consistently'.

The resources which were poured in to build new factories and other fixed capital assets were not matched in real value by the goods that were made available to the domestic market and export. The money generated by the construction and operation of new, unprofitable enterprises was pressing on the markets, creating a dangerously inflationary situation. In a relative freedom of movement, prices and incomes chased each other in a spiral. Inflation—too much money chasing too few goods—is a familiar phenomenon all over the communist world, except that in countries other than Yugoslavia inflation is usually suppressed, on the surface at least, by wages and prices being pegged. Yet goods which consumers want to buy are not there in sufficient quantities. A measure of inflation in those countries is the money paid for foreign-made goods in the black market, or for hard currency.

Even more serious than domestic inflation was Yugoslavia's balance of payments deficit which showed no signs of improvement. In 1964 matters came to a head. The balance of payments deficit in that year reached 166·6 million dollars and external debts rose beyond the 1,000 million dollar mark.

'We have been living beyond our means. Something very drastic must be done now to put things right,' a Yugoslav official explained to me late in 1964. The following year, in July, a sweeping new economic reform was instituted and the dinar was drastically devalued.

Enterprises were given further wide powers to dispose of their earnings but were told to rely on their own resources rather than on central funds. Banks were instructed to refuse credits to unprofitable businesses. Government departments had to put an end to all construction of new offices save those which were strictly necessary, and cut other expenditure.

The immediate result of the new measures was a sharp increase in prices, especially of food, consumer goods and rents. Some increase in the cost of living was expected. One of the purposes of the reform was precisely to tighten the belts of the consumers. Yet many prices rocketed far beyond the planned levels. In November 1965 I could see that most of the prices affecting ordinary people were about double what they had been during my previous visit only a year earlier. A pair of shoes which I bought for £1 in 1964 were now advertised at the equivalent of £2, in spite of the devaluation which had taken place in the meantime. A good meal cost me in Belgrade 15/- as compared to 10/- a year before.

Many foreign tourists who flocked to Yugoslavia in 1965 were disappointed by the high prices, although one purpose of the devaluation of the currency was precisely to attract more tourists. Yugoslavia, with its long, magnificent coast and wonderful Mediterranean climate by the Adriatic Sea, has been having more visitors than all the other communist countries put together. In 1965 the number of tourists was well over two million, representing a significant source of foreign exchange.

There was no corresponding increase in incomes for wide sections of the Yugoslav population and at no other time after the war had I heard people grumble more than during my visit in 1965. It should be borne in mind that most people employed in the public sector in Yugoslavia earned less than £14 a month, according to official statistics for September 1965.

But 1965 closed with a favourable trade balance for the first time in communist Yugoslavia. This was clearly an important success of the economic reform, although it remains to be seen if a continuous inflation of prices may not destroy the advantages which export industries initially derived from devaluation. But a new regulation by which exporting enterprises receive a greater share of their foreign exchange earnings should continue to stimulate exporters. The stagnation of imports in 1965, however, may well be a temporary matter due largely to exceptional measures by the authorities to cut down purchases abroad, including imports of essential raw materials and equipment.

* * *

The crucial question now is whether the Yugoslav leaders are willing, or able, to close down all, or most, of the uneconomic projects. By the end of 1965 there were some signs of reductions of the labour force, but there was clearly no large-scale dismissal of unproductive labour or closing down of enterprises. Hundreds of thousands of 'peasant-workers' who have been crowding industrial establishments are a burden to the national economy. But a senior Yugoslav official said to me in Belgrade, 'You cannot send a man

34

home to his village easily after he has become accustomed to the city air'.

It is obvious that the problem of unemployment (already quite serious, with something like 7 per cent of the labour force being in search of jobs during 1965) would become much more acute if only financially sound business were allowed to go on. Powerful pressures are applied behind the scenes to prevent any large-scale redundancies, even if temporarily imperative for reasons of national economy.

Luckily for Yugoslavia, doors are wide open in Western Europe to any workers who wish to go there. By 1966 about 250,000 Yugoslavs, travelling on regular passports, were employed in Western Germany, Sweden and other non-communist European countries. Of all the favourable aspects of Titoism, as distinct from other brands of communism, the freedom for most Yugoslavs to travel abroad, and if they wish, to take up employment there, is probably the most precious.*

The way the Yugoslav authorities allow their citizens to travel abroad is a practical manifestation of flexible and pragmatic attitudes prevailing in Belgrade. This, and indeed many other instances, show that the Yugoslav leaders often mean what they say when they lay stress on the need to bring out the humanitarian element in Marxism and socialism.

Refusal to be bound by the letter of Marxist-Leninist dogma has been described by some as the most endearing trait of Titoist communism. To be sure, the Yugoslav communists continue to insist that all their measures and reforms are fully in accord with that 'creative Marxism' which the founding fathers—Marx, Engels and Lenin—recommended. But there can be no doubt that by insisting on profitability of economic enterprise and on financial profit and gain as the indicator of economic success and its reward the Yugoslav communists have shifted their ground considerably. They

* This freedom has now been somewhat restricted, and some people—notably sons and daughters of war veterans—can more easily obtain permission to leave the country than others.

were the first in the communist world to pay open tribute to economic laws and try and do something about changing a system which had scorned such laws. By doing this they have made possible a fruitful dialogue with non-Marxists outside Yugoslavia. There can be no doubt that it is far easier for a non-communist Westerner to talk to a Yugoslav communist than to any other Marxist-Leninist.

Yet one can easily see that not all people who matter in Yugoslavia have been really convinced that the new policies are right. Many see in them a threat to their own positions of influence, a fear that may well be justified. At all events, it is obvious that Yugoslavia reformers often face bitter opposition within the ranks of the League of Communists.

These disagreements inside the League of Communists, with strong overtones of a naked struggle for Marshal Tito's succession, were dramatically illustrated when Alexander Rankovich, vice-President and in charge of the Security Service, as well as a large number of others, were dismissed or resigned last summer. These events may well foreshadow a further liberalisation of life in Yugoslavia, although the League of Communists is unlikely to give up its monopoly of political power.

That dogmatic attitudes can still gain the upper hand is perhaps most evident—and certainly most disastrous—in agriculture. Wisely, the Yugoslav communists in the early fifties allowed their peasants to leave the hated collectives into which they had previously been pushed. But subsequent attempts to aid the peasants through co-operative organisations seem to have been frustrated by those who dislike private property of any nature, but especially of land.

'We want to expand the public sector in our farming,' a member of the Yugoslav government explained to me when I interviewed him in the magnificent new building of the Federal Executive Council, outside Belgrade, late in 1965.

'But has not the experience in other socialist countries demonstrated the disastrous fallacy of orthodox communism in farming?'

36

'You think of the Russian *sovkhozes* and *kolkhozes*. Yugoslav socialised farms are very different from that. They are self-governing establishments in which workers are paid fair rewards for their labour. If you wish, we shall make arrangements for you to see one of these farms.'

The farm I saw was in Vojvodina, the most fertile region of Yugoslavia. It had about 25,000 acres and permanently employed over 2,000 workers. The establishment was said to be controlled by a 'workers' council'. But the man who clearly mattered most was the director, a suave person of city manners. Workers were paid more than average industrial employees were receiving. Yields of wheat were over 40 quintals a hectare. ('The best German farmer here could not get more than half of that before the war,' the director said.) Cows were giving over 20 pints of milk a day. The farm was well mechanised and fertilisers and other modern methods, most of them borrowed from the West and only a few from Russia, were applied. Attached to the farm was a meat-processing factory which exported a good deal of its ham, bacon and sausages to Britain.

Yet socialised holdings account for only about 13 per cent of the arable land, and many do not reach such high standards as the one I had seen at Banski Karlovci. Indeed it is an open secret that many Yugoslav nationalised farms are only kept alive by generous Government subsidies and that very often the yields achieved are not in proportion to the large capital investments made.

In Belgrade I was told that the Yugoslav Government would like to attract British companies to help run some of the farms with modern equipment and chemicals, sell the produce jointly with the Yugoslavs in Britain, and share the profit. This would apply specifically to maize growing. If this could be achieved it would certainly mark a new departure in business co-operation between the capitalist West and eastern Europe.

However, most of the 50 per cent or so of the population of Yugoslavia who are still earning their living largely by farming are independent peasants. It is clear that for some time to come at any rate they will hold the key to Yugoslavia's economic prosperity. 'If we could only produce enough wheat to cover our domestic needs we would be a long way towards solving our balance of payments problem,' a Yugoslav official said to me. 'But', he added, 'no socialist country has yet solved its farming problem. We haven't either.'

It is clear that the Yugoslav peasant has had the dirty end of the stick for a very long time now. It is perhaps encouraging and the sign of a new wind of change that this is now often admitted in the Yugoslav press. 'We have been paying our farmers disgracefully low prices for their produce,' said a reader's letter in a Yugoslav newspaper recently. The 'co-operatives', which were meant to help the peasant, monopolised their rights to purchase products from peasants and generally acted like 'large capitalist businesses bent on exploiting both their suppliers and buyers', as a Yugoslav source has put it.

A healthy agriculture and prosperous farmers would not only give the country sufficient food, it would also provide a growing market for Yugoslav industrial products and consumer goods. The importance of making farming attractive is particularly topical now when it would be desirable if unproductive industrial workers were to return to their villages. Yet at the moment of writing a Yugoslav peasant is still not allowed to buy himself a new tractor, although he may purchase a second-hand one, as indeed many have recently done. One still finds people of authority in Yugoslavia who take the view that peasants should not be permitted to earn more than is needed to cover elementary requirements. Such people believe that any surplus earned by the peasant should be promptly mopped up by taxation, as indeed it often is. 'If the peasant earns too much he doesn't want to work more,' a Yugoslav official said to me.

But such attitudes are now less frequent than they were in the past. Many Yugoslav communists see, and openly say so, that such views are incompatible with the plan to make good husbandry prevail in all fields. The latest trends seem to be favourable to the farmer. There is now serious talk that the maximum acreage allowed to be owned by independent farmers should be raised from the present much too low level of 25 acres. One can also see that independent craftsmen are getting more favourable treatment by the authorities. Private enterprise has been given some scope in tourism and catering. On strictly economic grounds there is a great deal to be said in favour of further expansion of the private sector. If pragmatism prevails in Belgrade such expansion seems inevitable.

2

The Wayward Satellites

Poland, Rumania, Bulgaria

I VISITED POLAND for the first time in 1960. I was then on my way by bus with a group of western tourists from Ostend to Moscow. It was the first time any one of us had been in the Soviet bloc proper. When we reached Poznan, in western Poland, we took advantage of the short stop there to rush through this somewhat forbidding-looking town of Germanic architecture, examining shop windows and comparing prices. In a café I asked a Polish girl if she liked the Russians. The question must have come to my mind because I had heard so much about the Polish October, in 1956, and the dislike of the Poles for the Russians. 'I love them so much I would drown them all in here,' she said, lifting her teaspoon. She spoke loudly. People at other tables turned round and laughed heartily.

Later I heard other Poles making the same kind of remark. Our official guide in Warsaw, an elderly lady, pointed her finger at the towering, wedding-cake style House of Culture, a gift from Russia, and said, 'See how hideous it is'. She made other disparaging comments when our bus passed the Soviet Embassy.

* * *

Poland may be a somewhat exaggerated case. The history of the Poles is filled with battles and rebellions against the Russians. One of the reasons why communism could never take deep roots in pre-war Poland was the widespread dislike of anything Russian.

The feelings were mutual. A few years before the war the entire leadership of the Polish Communist Party was apparently put to death on Stalin's order. Subsequently, in 1938, the Polish Communist Party was formally dissolved by the Soviet dictator. In the war against Germany, Polish communists made up some ground at home. But their resistance movement was of small consequence compared to that which was organised and led from London by nationalists. However, it is quite inconceivable that communism would have spread anywhere west of Russia but for the military might and political impact of the triumphant Soviet Union led by one of the most able and ruthless politicians of all times—Josef Stalin. There were countries where communism was brought to power on Russian bayonets even more blatantly than in Poland: Eastern Germany, Hungary, Rumania, Bulgaria. But these had been part of the defeated world. The Poles were allies who had contributed tremendous sacrifices for the common cause.

Any traveller in eastern Europe will soon see that Russians are not particularly popular anywhere, not even in Yugoslavia, Czechoslovakia or Bulgaria, where pan-Slav sentiments were exceptionally strong in the past. 'You will find that the Russians are liked best in those countries where they have never been, or stayed only a short time,' a young Rumanian diplomat told me.

Everywhere in eastern Europe, and this is also true of such

western republics of the USSR as Lithuania, Latvia and Estonia and the Ukraine, the Russians proper are regarded as uncouth and primitive, if basically good-natured and hospitable as well as talented in their own way. But they are definitely not something worth imitating. And I saw very few people in eastern Europe who said they would like to visit the Soviet Union. Many said they wished to visit London or Paris. The lack of attraction of things Russian must have been one of the great weaknesses of the post-war Soviet 'empire' in eastern Europe.

Conversely, the mistrust with which the Russians customarily look on the outside world is only a shade less pronounced when it is directed at 'people's democracies' in eastern Europe. When our bus—in 1960—finally reached the Soviet frontier I noticed with surprise the same kind of watchtowers on the other side as marked the Iron Curtain in central Europe. Across the bridge were the Soviet Union and the peak-capped, jackbooted guards.

'Do you have any contacts with the men on the other side?' I asked a Polish frontier guard. 'Any joint parties, meetings, discussion groups?'

'None whatsoever', he replied. 'We never go there. They never come to us.'

Peasants living in the bordering region had to obtain visas through long-winded processes if they wished to visit their relatives and friends on the other side of the frontier. Very few on the Polish side had been across since the war. I found a similar situation at the Soviet frontier with Rumania in 1965. Yet there are nearly three million Rumanians living on the other side, in territories annexed by the Soviet Union on the basis of a pact made with Hitler in 1939.

If communism has swept over eastern Europe largely because of the military impact, direct or indirect, of the Soviet Union, it has become equally clear that most of the régimes there survive only because of the Soviet military presence or threat of intervention. This became acutely evident in 1956, with the uprisings in Poland and shortly afterwards in Hungary.

It was the Hungarian revolution which really marked a watershed in the contemporary life of the eastern European nations. 'Don't expect us to start a revolution,' a Rumanian anti-communist said to me when I last visited Bucharest in November 1965. 'We remember Hungary'.

The Hungarian uprising, which ended by being crushed by Soviet tanks, was an end of an era to all those who had hoped for a violent upheaval and total liberation from communism in eastern Europe. But it also caused a profound shock in communist circles, in Moscow and elsewhere. It became clear to all far-sighted Marxist-Leninists that communism could only remain a living force in eastern Europe if wedded to nationalism. This could not fail to have important repercussions for the Soviet bloc and its cohesion. Long suppressed yet always present and powerful feelings of nationalism now emerged into the open, albeit under a Marxist-Leninist garb, and the 'monolithic community of brotherly socialist nations' began to change and disintegrate, a process which continues.

In Poland, communism would have been swept away like a pack of cards in October 1956 but for the threat of Russian armed intervention. Yet, the man who emerged as the new leader of communist Poland, Wladyslaw Gomulka, who had himself been victimised for his 'nationalist deviations', succeeded in gaining a measure of acceptance by the Polish people. Frugal, abstemious, pedantic, yet unassuming and in his own way genuinely concerned with the welfare of his people, Gomulka is regarded by many Poles as a lesser evil. 'I like the way he walks about in Warsaw parks, without any guards, just like any one of us,' a Pole said to me when I visited the country more extensively in 1963.

By then many of the more sensational gains of the October upheaval had already been whittled down. While keeping his ear to the ground for any signs of violent discontent of the people in his charge, Gomulka was not slow in clamping down on developments that might seriously undermine the monopoly of power of the Communist Party. Workers' councils, introduced in 1956, on the Yugoslav model, would no doubt have resulted in considerably greater industrial democracy than they did in Yugoslavia, as the communists in Poland were too weak to manipulate such institutions from behind the scenes. So a direct assault was made on these councils. They were first infiltrated by communists in 1957, and by 1958 the entire system was changed so that the communist organisation in the industrial enterprises was given full formal rights to be able to dominate the workers' councils. Consequently these became of little significance as instruments of the workers for the fulfilment of their rights and ambitions.

In 1963 I could see a remarkable decline of the spirit of provocative non-conformism for which Poland had previously been known. Life in students' clubs and cabarets, which earlier had been bristling with irreverence and political satire, was now only a pale shadow of its former self. I visited the famous 'Krokodil' cabaret one night, in Warsaw's Old Town, looking for lively, politically-minded young people offering interesting comments or engaging in flamboyant discussions. I saw a middle-aged man singing a lugubrious Russian love song accompanying himself on a balalaika. Several couples were already under the influence of drink and were petting clumsily and talking incoherently in the dark, cave-like premises of the cabaret.

The communist officials one talked to were sophisticated, debonair and self-confident. They were trying to convey the impression that they were doing what they had to do only reluctantly, vaguely in disagreement with communist dogmas, yet subscribing to them in practice for some undefined patriotic reason. This was also true of the slick young linguists who presided over student organisations. They already had all the makings of the men of the New Class. These students' organisations are extremely important bodies, deciding on many practical issues which affect the everyday life of students, such as scholarships, accommodation, holiday work and even employment.

I heard at that time that intellectuals in Poland were under a cloud and expressionist and other non-representational painters were having their State grants refused. The new line was coming from Moscow and the Polish communists had apparently been told by the Russians to try to enforce a stricter 'cultural policy'. Meetings were held all over Poland, explaining the need for the Poles not to diverge too much from the Russian practices in intellectual and artistic life. It was clear that belonging to the 'socialist' world headed by Moscow set limits to the freedom of the Poles to proceed on their own 'road to socialism'.

Still, Warsaw was doing its best to live up to its reputation of being the 'eastern Paris'. However drab in comparison to Western cities, life in the Polish capital was far more free and gay than in Moscow. Travel to Poland began to be regarded by the Russians, and others in the communist world, as a kind of second-best when it was not possible to go beyond the Iron Curtain. 'My father died in Paris as a White Guard exile,' a member of a Soviet economic delegation said to me in Warsaw. 'I shall never be allowed to travel outside the socialist world. But I can go to Poland—and I enjoy myself here', he said.

*   *   *

In the packed restaurants of the international hotels in Warsaw Russian-made champagne flowed freely and tables were laden with expensive food. The music being played was the latest Western hits. Smartly dressed local girls waiting to be picked up by foreigners were numerous. One encounter might bring them more than they earned as typists in an entire month.

Incidentally, people who ought to know agree that a lonely businessman can pick up a 'good-time girl' more easily in eastern Europe, and at far less expense, than in London, in spite of the puritanical pretensions of most communist régimes. To be sure, the girls who hang around international

44

hotels are a tiny, insignificant minority. This is true of every communist country I visited, including Cuba, which has State-run brothels. But coloured students at the Lumumba University in Moscow told me that promiscuity was rife in Russia among young women and girls living on inadequate scholarships, or working in offices for monthly salaries which equal the price of two pairs of shoes of mediocre quality.

Also, in Warsaw at that time, hard currency notes could be exchanged for *zlotys* at three times the official tourist rate simply by handing the money to any waiter in an international hotel.

One important gain of the Polish people after the October events in 1956 has stayed almost intact. As distinct from other members of the Soviet bloc, Poland's agriculture is largely in the hands of independent smallholders. And it appears that this accounts for the absence of such acute shortages as are familiar elsewhere in the communist world. It is believed that Polish peasants manage to take out more from an acre of their land than farmers in other countries of the Soviet orbit, although farming in Poland is primitive and inefficient compared to Western standards. The horse is still by far the most important mode of traction.

When Polish farmers were left free to leave and disband their collectives after the change of government in 1956 the opportunity was promptly seized. 'But don't you think the authorities might try collectivisation again?' I asked a Polish farmer in 1963, remembering a conversation the previous day with a leading economist in Warsaw. To *him* the present was only a temporary phase and full socialisation of the land on the Soviet model was the ultimate goal in Poland too.

'No, there is no fear of that', the Polish farmer replied. 'Nobody wants it here, and there are no communists in our village or anywhere near.'

Indeed what I found most astonishing was this absence of

45

communist agitators over wide regions of the Polish country-side.* The authority, in spiritual and many other matters in Poland, seemed to be firmly vested in the Roman Catholic Church and its clergy, led by the able, patriotic and forthright Cardinal Stefan Wyszinski.

Some 90 per cent of the population in Poland are believed to be avowed Christians. Official enquiries at universities revealed that even among students the proportion of practising Catholics was over 60 per cent! It is clear that in the battle for the minds of the people the Polish communists have been strikingly unsuccessful. In fact, religion remains a strong social force in all eastern Europe, although percentages of those who actually practise their religion vary from country to country and are probably nowhere as high as in Poland. But even in Russia, where exceptional efforts have been made by the communists to eradicate religion by massive atheist propaganda and compulsory closure of churches and priests' seminaries, Christian faith is a significant social phenomenon, especially among the womenfolk.

It is now clear that communism with all its powerful apparatus of propaganda and compulsion cannot in the long run supersede religion. On the contrary, many people in communist countries turn to the Church who might not have done so under other circumstances. This explains, perhaps, the unusual strength of some Christian Churches in the communist world, which in its turn gives church leaders there exceptional self-confidence and imbues them with a sense of mission which sometimes leads to intransigence and intolerance. For example, the teaching of the Roman Catholic Church on birth control seems to be taken more seriously by people in Poland than in other Catholic countries, which also provides one of the constant sources of discord with the Warsaw Government as the very high birth rate and excessive growth

* In 1961, there was no Party organisation in 1,600 Polish villages. Out of 11·5 million farmers only 160,000 were members of the Communist Party. See *The Independent Satellite* by Hansjakob Stehle, Pall Mall Press, London, 1965, pp. 14 and 125.

of the population tend to wipe out all the fruits of progress in the supplies of food, consumer goods and housing.

I vividly remember a visit I paid to Lovicz, a small pilgrimage town near Warsaw, during my visit to Poland in 1963. In the main church, a large baroque structure, masses of country people were pressing towards the altar and the shouts of the priest from the pulpit, urging the crowd to be more disciplined, were drowned in the tumult. Outside, upwards from a thousand men and women, many of them young, were crowding at the main door, ready to pour in when the church reopened and a new Mass began. Most of the young men wore immaculate black suits and white shirts and many of the women and girls wore the customary rainbow-coloured, plaited skirts. There were long rows of motor-cycles along a nearby wall, but most of the congregation seemed to have arrived on horse carts. Behind the church, an obelisk to the memory of the Soviet Army stood isolated, like a sore thumb. On roads and country lanes little chapels, some of them very ornate, were decorated with fresh flowers and lights were burning in stained-glass lamps.

* * *

With Andrzey, a student from Warsaw University who was helping me out in Polish, I walked for miles to reach what I wanted to see: a typical Polish village. We passed by numerous typical Polish ponds with geese splashing about and waded sometimes ankle deep in mud. When we reached the village we had no difficulty in finding peasants who were ready to talk to us. We established ourselves in a large kitchen which was soon filled with farmers and their wives, and many faces of young children were pressing tight against the window pane from outside.

This was a twelve-acre holding. There were altogether about 200 households in the village, none farming more than 25 acres of land. Twelve acres was about average. In normal times, the peasant said, he could break even and perhaps save a little. But this year was bad. Heavy rains in the previous autumn and a disastrous winter had badly affected the crops.

47

'We have nothing to feed our pigs', the wife said. They were wondering if they had enough to feed themselves. 'It's difficult to buy food around here,' the farmer said. I asked him if this was different before the war, in non-communist times. 'Yes,' he said. 'Then you could buy anything you wanted.' 'But,' his wife put in, 'you had to have the money, and few of us had it.'

When harvests were good the farm might bring a gross income of about £580 a year (at the tourist rate of exchange). Of this about one-tenth went in taxes. A large part of the food grown on the farm was consumed by the farmer and his family. From the rest, a certain proportion had to be delivered to the State at prices about one-third of the free market level. On this farm compulsory deliveries included about 10 cwt. of wheat, 17 cwt. of potatoes and 4 cwt. of pork. Any surplus was sold in the nearest town by the farmer himself or members of the family. There were four head of cattle on the farm, one horse, ten pigs, six sheep and a number of poultry. The family provided all the labour.

Little investment was made on the farm, as savings were small even in the best of years. In theory, long-term loans could be obtained from the National Bank at 3 per cent interest for periods of up to twenty years, but—the farmer explained—such loans were difficult to come by in practice. It was easier to obtain credit facilities from a local co-operative bank which made loans for periods of up to 15 months at between 3 and 5 per cent interest.

'Thank God we are all in good health,' said the farmer. Illness in the family could spell disaster as private farmers were not covered by the National Health Service. Hospital cost about 15s. a day and a visit by a doctor nearly 7s.

Life as painted to me by the farmers in this village was clearly precarious. But it was certainly more prosperous than on any of the collective or State farms I had seen in Poland or anywhere else in the Soviet bloc, including Russia itself.

One could see no obvious signs of poverty in this Polish village. Many of the low, thatched-roof cottages had been freshly decorated with blue paint, and they looked neat and trim. Clean yellow curtains in the small windows added a touch of gaiety. Children were well dressed, most of them wearing shoes although it was quite warm, and they played with modern toys. Some farmhouses looked quite prosperous. Perhaps this was due to the opportunities of part-time employment in a nearby brickworks. But several families in the village were receiving money and parcels from relatives in the USA and elsewhere in the West.

Some help to Polish peasants is provided by the co-operatives, or 'agrarian circles', which are fairly widespread in the country and are far more genuinely democratic organisations than similar bodies in other communist countries. In this village some 70 per cent of all the peasants were members of the local Circle, which provided them with machinery, better seeds, fertilisers and various services. The officers of the co-operative in the village seemed to have been freely elected and were trusted by the other peasants.

A ten-year old boy volunteered to take me round the village to look at machinery and implements which the Circle had recently acquired and which were now in use on the farms. These machines were hired by the peasants for specific operations in the fields, for a small fee. Non-members could also avail themselves of the services, but were charged 20 per cent more. There were tractors, multiple ploughs, threshing machines, a combine harvester and a number of heavy-duty trucks—all of Polish make and all apparently brand new. Facilities for garaging and maintenance were clearly inadequate, however. The little boy took obvious pride in his knowledge of exactly where the equipment happened to be in use, or lying about, that day. As we walked along, a number of other boys and girls joined us, and we soon made quite a procession.

There are very few collective farms in Poland now. Most of the 'socialised' land—which constitutes about 10 per cent of the total—belongs to State farms, or Russian-type *sovkhozes*. Such State farms are often supposed to act as models for the rest of the farming in their areas.

From the village where we were it took me and Andrzey threequarters of an hour to reach the nearest State farm. Again we walked along rutted village tracks, through a country which was flat and unlovely, save for groves of tall and slender birch trees with storks nesting in their tops.

The buildings on the State farm seemed to have been recently constructed. Children played cowboys and Indians in front of a large, squat structure which housed the State-appointed director of the farm and other officers and their families. A few hundred yards away, the farm labourers lived in a row of identical houses, small and dull, a cross between the huts in a concentration camp and the humbler council houses of a London suburb.

A girl of twelve, precocious and frail, smiled at us when we expressed the wish to talk with her parents and led us inside the house. In the living-room there were more children, some crawling about on the floor, and there were numerous crosses and religious pictures on the walls, which indeed was the same in every Polish home I visited.

'If only I had the house to myself,' the wife sighed. She, her husband and five children shared the dwelling with another family, who had four children. The life of these people was grim, far grimmer than anything I had seen before in Poland. Both the man and his wife worked on the State farm for a combined income of just over £175 a year. But a suit of clothes of indifferent quality cost about £28 and a pair of shoes over £4, and a pound of pork nearly 10s.

I asked the couple how often they ate meat, and they laughed bitterly. 'Once a month at the most,' the wife said. I was told that they could buy certain food from the farm at reduced prices. They had sufficient milk, bread and potatoes—their staples. They were not actually starving, but it was clear to me that they and their children were badly undernourished.

'You can see why our peasants don't like socialism,' Andrzey said as we left the place. It is plain that such State farms cannot really be efficient, because productivity is inevitably low when labour is undernourished. In the Soviet Union the position is even worse than in Poland. Such *sovkhozes*, how-ever, provide a means by which the Government can get some-thing out of the people for next to nothing; they are a way to create that 'surplus value' out of which more ambitious schemes of industrial construction can be financed. The State farm I saw in Poland—and indeed such farms elsewhere, in-cluding the USSR—struck me as a very good example of what the Marxists call 'exploitation of man by man'.

Most communists, however, look at the system of State farms as an ideal arrangement which will eventually replace all other, intermediary, solutions. State farms are preferred because they are closest to the traditional Marxist-Leninist vision whereby agriculture is run on the principles applied in industrial factories. It is only for reasons of expediency, there-fore, that the other forms are admitted, including smallhold-ings in private hands. The *kolkhoz*, or collective farm, is also regarded as a temporary expedient as it in fact entails a good deal of 'private enterprise' and may represent a considerable element of uncertainty in a system which is supposed to be governed by detailed, rational planning.

I have seen 'collectives' which did not appear too unbear-able to their members, although experience in eastern Europe has abundantly demonstrated that farmers prefer to work their own farms if they are allowed to do so. Collective farms are perhaps at their best when peasants have had no long tradition of personal ownership of land, or have relatively fresh memories of virtual serfdom, which existed in some eastern European countries until fairly recently. Moreover, the management of the *kolkhoz* must be in the hands of a chairman who knows his job and is trusted by the members. Finally, due account must be taken of the natural desire of the peasants to have at least some land of their own; and of course, they must be assured a fair share in the total harvest achieved by the collec-tive.

It appears that few collective farms in the communist world fulfil these conditions. At all events, even the most satisfactory collective farm entails a large measure of exploitation of labour, as the products of the *kolkhoz* are all sold to State agencies at prices which are invariably a good deal lower than those of the free market.

*   *   *

When I visited Rumania, late in 1965, I inspected a large collective farm in a village in the Danube Delta. In Rumania, most of the farms in the socialist sector—some 85 per cent—are collectives. The soil was somewhat more fertile than the average in Rumania, and the chairman of the *kolkhoz*, a burly man in his fifties, was also a Member of Parliament, which indicated that he was a better farming manager than most and a trusted communist. He was clearly a man who knew his business. With the help of an interpreter, we went carefully through his books and he talked frankly about his problems. But he concluded: 'This year our members should be earning a good deal more than last.' He claimed that if all went well each of the 6,000 or so households in the collective would be netting about £160 on average by the end of the year, in cash and distributed produce. This was much (about a third) above the average for Rumanian *kolkhozes*. In addition, each household in the collective was allowed to own a maximum of three-quarters of an acre of its own land. 'In principle no household may have more than one cow,' the chairman said. 'But we don't really bother if they keep two or three.' The main problem was how to keep a reasonable balance between what a member did in the collective fields and what he did on his own plot.

There were some 300 cows in a new shed. It was all quite clean, if primitive. 'We have only begun with the mechanisation on our farm,' the chairman explained. On average, about 16 pints of milk a day could be obtained from a cow.

We later visited the members in their homes, neat little cottages with exquisitely carved window frames and cornices. 'Before the Revolution,' an old lady explained in the presence of my interpreter, 'my husband was a sharecropper. He worked for a landlord and received only one-third of the crop he harvested. There was no electricity in this house then.'

Perhaps conditions of collectivisation are more favourable in Rumania than elsewhere; perhaps the communist régime is more flexible and better able to bring into harmony the interests of the peasants and those of the State. Rumania is certainly about the only country in eastern Europe which has not only been consistently self-sufficient in food but manages to export considerable quantities of farm produce.

Yet Rumanian officials themselves admitted to me that their agriculture too was a weak link in the national plans as targets of food production were often not met. In Rumanian towns the food I saw in the shops or in the open peasant markets was of poor quality and very expensive. Moreover, many of the food items, such as meat, bread or cheese, were double in price since I had last visited Rumania, in 1961, when collectivisation was not yet completed.

It is interesting that Khrushchev is reported to have criticised the Rumanians in 1961 for their eagerness to collectivise their farming, pointing to the failures of socialist agriculture in the Soviet Union.

This is believed to have been the first open clash between Khrushchev and the Rumanian leader, the late Gheorghiu-Dej, after relations between the two countries had been deteriorating for some time. This Russo-Rumanian dispute is now regarded as one of the most significant developments in eastern Europe of recent times. It marked a reassertion of economic nationalism, which spelled the end to Khrushchev's grandiose plan for a rational division of labour in the Soviet bloc according to which each country would concentrate on the production of goods for which it was deemed to be most suitable.

There was a good deal of sense in this Russian suggestion. It was made, no doubt, because the constant propping of eastern European economies became a serious burden and a source of considerable potential danger to the Russians. The eastern European economies had all been developing according to the Soviet Stalinist pattern. Each of these countries insisted on having its own heavy industry as a basis and tried to turn out a wide range of sophisticated manufactured products. These ambitions often led to absurd situations when the imports needed to produce certain products, e.g. steel, were actually more expensive than the value of the final output. It would naturally have been better if only one or two countries in the bloc concentrated on developing steel and other such industries,—East Germany, Czechoslovakia and Poland, perhaps. But this would have meant that there would be no heavy industry for the others. 'They wanted us to be just peasants,' a Rumanian summed up the situation when I talked to him in a train during a recent visit.

The Rumanians are now building the largest steelworks in Europe—scheduled to produce between four and five million tons of ingot steel annually. Much of the equipment for the Galati project has been provided by an Anglo-French consortium. The Russians had promised to supply the slabbing mill. But at the time when I visited the building site, in November 1965, the contract with the Russians had still not been signed.

The idea for a close economic integration of the Soviet bloc was born in 1957, after disastrous dislocations following the events in Poland and Hungary in the previous year. The Council for Mutual Economic Assistance—the CMEA or COMECON—was revived for the purpose. Set up originally as a counterpart to the Western European economic organisation under the Marshall Plan, the CMEA led an uneventful existence until Khrushchev began to regard it as a vehicle for his plan of a supranational authority which would put right the somewhat anarchic conditions in eastern Europe's economic life.

By 1961 the announcement was made that the CMEA was moving towards international authority. But then reports also began to reach the West of serious disagreements among the members of the association. These reports coincided with the growing conflict between China and Russia. It is difficult to imagine that the Rumanian Government, which had so far been noted for its unquestioned subservience to the Soviet Union, would have resisted the Russian plans, as it in fact did, had the Rumanians not been aware of the exceptional difficulties in which Moscow found itself on account of its dispute with Peking.

The matter came to a head in 1962 when the Russians and some of their eastern European satellites, notably the East Germans, Czechs and Poles (who would presumably profit most by a division of labour in the Soviet bloc) were pressing hard in favour of economic and industrial integration under the auspices of the CMEA and criticising the Rumanians for their obstreperous attitude. By 1963 it became clear that the Rumanians had won their point and the project for a supra-national authority was shelved. Yet there can be little doubt that if the Rumanians had not torpedoed Khrushchev's plan somebody else would have. As one authority on the subject, David Floyd, has put it: 'None of the countries of eastern Europe would have gained in the long run from becoming just a part of an unwieldy economic empire directed from Moscow, which is what Khrushchev's plans would have meant.'*

*   *   *

There is no doubt that at the moment of writing the most loyal satellite of Russia, perhaps the only satellite in the true sense of the word, is Bulgaria, a small Balkan country bordering on Yugoslavia and Rumania, with both of which she has been embroiled in bitter disputes and rivalry in the past. With some claims to a position of pre-eminence in the Balkan peninsula in the past, Bulgaria had the misfortune to back the wrong horse in both world wars. Her influence had consequently been much reduced, which never ceased to rankle in the hearts of Bulgarian patriots. There has always been a strong pro-Russian undercurrent in Bulgaria, which is peopled by Slavs of Greek Orthodox faith. Moreover the Russians did much in the nineteenth century to liberate the Bulgarians from the Turkish yoke. Although allied to Germany in the last war the Bulgarian Government refused to declare war on the

* *Rumania: Russia's Dissident Ally,* by David Floyd (Pall Mall Press, London, 1965), p. 81.

USSR, but that did not prevent the Russians from declaring war on Bulgaria and subsequently treating her as one of the defeated German satellites. In the wake of the Soviet Army a communist régime was set up which savagely repressed all democratic freedoms and opposition. The régime has also ruthlessly nipped in the bud any attempt by more independent-minded Bulgarian communists to steer a course that would be less subservient to the USSR.

When I stepped out of my train in Sofia on a rainy October day in 1962 I found the scene strangely familiar. I had been here in this same railway station just over 24 years earlier. And I now noticed with surprise that the old, smoky building was hardly changed at all, except that the passing of the years showed in more peeling paint on the walls and more missing or broken window panes. It is interesting that railway modernisation has rarely fired the imagination of communist planners. While air transport and bus services have made remarkable headway almost everywhere in the communist world railways have been sadly neglected, in the Soviet Union as much as elsewhere.

I left the railway station and entered the familiar cobbled square, looking for a taxi. There was no such thing to be had. A friendly railway porter, a young buxom girl, advised me to walk on and join the bus queue near by, in which some 200 men and women already stood in pouring rain.

Then, suddenly, a small middle-aged man carrying an open umbrella approached me with a friendly smile. Was I a stranger in town? Was it my first visit to Bulgaria? Could he help me to carry my luggage? He was no spiv, loafer or beggar—these are rare in communist countries. Whoever he was, I thought, I would follow my usual principle when travelling in the communist world: always be friendly and communicative, if mildly puzzled, whenever approached by anybody.

I still don't know what Mr Panchev really was or what were his motives. By the way he talked he seemed to be a part-time government propagandist. He said he was a post office clerk on holiday. He certainly had an astonishing command of

56

statistics at his finger tips. He said he would be most ready to meet me again and show me around Sofia. I had few friends in the Bulgarian capital and I took full advantage of his offer. He might have been an agent of the Security Service, for all I knew. Or maybe he was just a charitable man wishing to help a stranger. Perhaps he was both. He was certainly very useful on that wet evening of my arrival when he accompanied me to an hotel, and on many subsequent days. When we parted, he gave me a souvenir—a lighter made in China—and I still have it.

The following day we walked in the main square of the city and Panchev pointed out a large building in front of which a soldier dressed in an oddly ornate uniform was marching up and down 'This is where the great Dimitrov is lying,' Panchev said. Dimitrov, who won fame for defying Goering at the German Reichstag fire trial in the thirties and is regarded as the father of Bulgarian communism, was, for most of his active life, a faithful and able international agent of Stalin.

I scarcely recognised Sofia which I had known 24 years before. A great many buildings have been constructed in the centre of the town, in dull, heavy style. When I had last seen Sofia it was a lively small city, with officers in white peaked caps, large epaulettes on their shoulders and floating capes, strolling elegantly on the boulevards; with groups of people gathered at street corners, gesticulating and quarrelling loudly; with many taverns and bars where musicians would often strike up a patriotic tune and the guests would stand, drink, and hurl their glasses against the wall. There were many groups and societies, some of which were illegal, but most of them dedicated to the patriotic aim of greater Bulgaria.

Contrary to what we had been told in Yugoslav schools, King Boris was, to all appearances, genuinely popular. When a friend of mine made a disparaging remark about him in a tavern in Sofia, we had difficulty in getting away safely from angry locals. Excitement was in the air in that summer of 1939 and there was a promise of better things to come. This was rather typical of most eastern European capitals. Everywhere people, especially the young, felt that changes were on the way which would remove the wrongs and stupidities of an age that had universally been regarded as unsatisfactory.

But now the crowds moving along the huge square by the Dimitrov Mausoleum looked drab, sullen and dull by comparison, although on the whole they looked better fed and better dressed. Somehow, oddly, they struck me as creatures deprived of their manhood, an impression I had of the crowds I mingled with in most communist cities I visited.

'See that hotel there,' Panchev said proudly. 'It was built entirely by Bulgarians, including its lifts with photo-electric cells.' Certainly the Hotel Ryle looked impressive and contemporary, and inside the furnishings were of good quality. We walked through shops in Sofia's main shopping centre. Nearly every product was made in Bulgaria, which also filled Panchev with pride, and I found similar sentiments in other Bulgarians, many of whom were by no means communist sympathisers. Prices corresponded to wages in roughly the ratio applicable elsewhere in eastern Europe, a man's suit of clothes, for example, costing about a month's wages. But quality was mediocre in most cases.

There were, however, acute shortages of many food items. Eggs were rare in Sofia and elsewhere in Bulgarian towns. Beans, a national staple, were unobtainable at the time. Butter was scarce and expensive. Prices of food and many other items in people's budgets had gone up by 30 and even 40 per cent since the previous spring.

'But now I want you to be my guest in my home,' Panchev said. Later that evening we both joined in a queue and waited for about an hour at a butcher's shop to buy 2 lb. of pork for our dinner.

He introduced me to his wife, his daughter and son. 'I would like you to tell my son', Panchev said, 'that he must learn and work hard in school in order to get ahead in the world, anywhere, under any régime.'

Panchev was a communist supporter from pre-war days, by no means a typical Bulgarian. The son was 16, a bright if somewhat frivolous boy. 'Why', he said, 'must we admire everything Russian? I can see that British and American cars are better than Soviet, and many other Western products are more practical and better designed than those made in the USSR. . . . In the last war Russia would have been beaten but for the Americans and the British. . . . We have many newspapers, but they all say the same things and often tell lies.'

'Do you listen to Western radio?' I asked.

'Yes, but only for jazz. All my friends listen too.'

'Would you say your views are typical among your friends at school?'

'Yes, certainly, we all think more or less in the same way.'

'This may be so,' the father interrupted, 'but most of you have joined the Brigade of Volunteers.' (This is a kind of auxiliary citizens' police set up on the Russian model to help control rowdies and hooligans.)

'We did that so we could get free tickets for films and football matches.'

'You see?' Panchev said to me. 'He doesn't appreciate what he has. Before the war we had much unemployment here and we were just a backward agricultural country.' Schooling was now universal and there were free health and other social services.

When we had left the flat and walked down the rickety staircase of the building in which the Panchev family lived, he said, 'I grant you one thing, though. You have free trade unions in the West and we haven't. I believe all these price increases would have been impossible in your country without a corresponding increase in wages. Another thing: too many of our communists just want money and power for themselves.'

*   *   *

Even Bulgaria has lately been showing signs of greater independence. Bulgarian representatives have been touring Western European capitals in search of more trade and technological co-operation. Mr George Thomson, the British Minister of State for Foreign Affairs, was given a chance to speak on television in Sofia during a visit there in October 1965. The welcome extended to him would have been unthinkable three years earlier. In the autumn of 1962, when I visited the Bulgarian capital, Western and also Yugoslav diplomats told me they had great difficulty in establishing any contacts with Bulgarians, communist or otherwise.

The wind of change in Sofia, which any visitor can detect, may be significant for another reason. It is not inconceivable that the Soviet Union itself suggested to the Bulgarian leaders that they might try and stand on their own feet rather than hold to Russia's apron strings all the time.

With their own plans for a tightly controlled, economically streamlined eastern Europe thwarted, the Russians may well be reluctant to face the prospect of underwriting indefinitely inefficient and unpopular régimes. By and large, Russia's policies in eastern Europe have brought her little benefit; especially since Stalin's death and the removal of the iron hand, crude economic exploitation of the region has ceased to be practicable. After all, the standard of living in every single eastern European country seems to be higher than in the Soviet Union itself. Besides, Soviet policies have brought much harm to the prestige of the USSR, which is parading elsewhere in the world as a champion of freedom and national emancipation. In eastern Europe Russia has been feared and disliked more than at any time in the past.

However, the Russians will no doubt continue to want harmless, if not always obedient neighbours. It is likely that for some time at any rate Moscow will regard as a minimum for its safety that the régimes in eastern Europe should remain communist. The reverberations of the Hungarian uprising in 1956, when for a moment it seemed that a communist régime could be overthrown by a few bold actions of the city populace, have been felt not only over the entire communist area in eastern Europe, but deep inside the Soviet Union as well. This was a traumatic experience for communists everywhere, and it was no coincidence that the Yugoslav communists, who had themselves a major share in releasing the spirit of rebellion, eventually endorsed the Russian action when the uprising was crushed by armed force. No matter what the domestic and external experiments of communist régimes in eastern Europe may be, they will continue to regard the Soviet might as the ultimate guarantor of their survival. This sets the limits to freedom in eastern Europe.

'I can now have a drink with you in this hotel,' an old friend of mine said in Bucharest during my last visit. 'This is a change. But it is not enough.' To him it was almost a betrayal of his ideals that one should bargain for so little. When I had met him in 1961 we had talked furtively. He looked over his shoulders for snoopers. But since then Rumania had had her quarrel with Russia and it was easy to see that things were changing in many ways. Thousands of political prisoners have been released. Jamming of foreign broadcasts had ceased. Rumania was increasingly looking to the West for inspiration and ideas. To me these seemed important changes with much promise for more reforms to follow.

'If we only had as much freedom as the Yugoslavs to travel abroad,' a student of economics at Bucharest University said to me. 'If only our farmers were as free as they are in Yugoslavia and if there were more competition among industrial enterprises and a better choice in the markets,' he added. He was not really opposed to the régime, or at any rate did not appear to be. In his opinion the emancipation of Rumania from the status of a colourless Russian satellite was in itself a very good thing and the Government deserved support for their courage.

The Rumanian communists, an unusually disciplined and able lot, are reluctant to experiment with their economic system. In this they differ from their communist neighbours, but it is not in itself proof that the orthodox communism practised in Rumania is succeeding where others have failed. The same problems are already appearing which have pushed others on the road of 'economic revisionism'.

Even in Bulgaria, the communists are now paying tribute to new ideas. In Czechoslovakia a reform is being introduced

61

which in many ways resembles some elements of the Yugoslav experiment. And Czechoslovakia at one time had the reputation of being a shop window of Soviet-type communism in central Europe. 'For us the new reform is a matter of life and death,' a senior Czechoslovak planning official told me recently.

The story is repeating itself in Hungary, Poland and East Germany. Everywhere the old 'command economy' has led to disastrous problems. In Czechoslovakia, for example, goods have been accumulating which could not be sold because of poor quality and at the same time severe shortages of the most elementary products persist.

Broadly, the new reforms give individual enterprises wider powers of decision, making financial profit an important criterion of efficiency, and they generally introduce a measure of competition in the market so that the quality of goods can be improved and costs of production reduced. It is now widely realised that men are consumers as well as producers and that to disregard the consumer indefinitely is self-defeating—unless strict methods of police terror are used, and this is no longer feasible in eastern Europe. It is particularly important that customers abroad should be satisfied. One important reason for the Czechoslovak reforms is that the country's exports have met with bitter criticism abroad.

People in eastern Europe have been disillusioned with Russia and her ways, not only ordinary people but most of the communists too. But the nations of eastern Europe have been disappointed with each other too. They now look increasingly to the advanced industrial nations in the West for the supply of equipment and technological know-how.

Russia will always retain some importance, as a market for second rate manufactured goods and a source of raw materials and foodstuffs. But the West can better supply such sophisticated plant, chemicals, and other products which eastern Europeans need in order to rise into the ranks of industrial nations proper, which they so much want to do. Yet in order to be able to buy these goods from the free world they must raise output and exports. In their efforts to achieve this they are finding the orthodox communist dogma a serious obstacle.

The Yugoslav example may have demonstrated that there is no easy way out, even for those who are prepared to go a very long way in experimenting with new approaches. To try to have the best of both worlds may sometimes mean falling between two stools. Yet in the opinion of many eastern Europeans today such experiments are a matter of necessity rather than choice. However, processes of economic experimentation and contacts with the free world inevitably generate internal changes of the régime, which should be welcomed by all who wish eastern Europeans to live a happier and fuller life.

3

The Motherland of Socialism

The USSR

THE LATE Sir Winston Churchill once said of Russia: 'It is a riddle wrapped up in mystery inside an enigma'. No doubt this is one of the reasons why the Soviet Union has managed to attract and fascinate so many people in Europe and elsewhere.

Before the last war people were largely ignorant of what really went on inside the Soviet Union. There was a great deal of literature on the subject, but one had no means of establishing what was true and what was false in these books, most of which had been written by people with axes to grind—communists or else communist defectors. Reports of inhuman forced labour camps, of police terror and degradingly low living standards of most of the people in Stalin's Russia could be dismissed as 'capitalist fabrications'—and no one knew for certain if they were or not.

This is no longer quite so. The Russian leaders and authorities have themselves been more truthful and informative of late than in the past. Western people can now travel more easily to the Soviet Union. Many journalists have been there and the picture of drab crowds in Russian towns and shoddy goods in shops is well established. Many foreigners have studied at Russian universities. The knowledge of the Russian language among Western visitors is now less rare than it used to be.

Yet with all the improvement that has come about in mutual contacts one of the most striking facts about Russia is still the prevailing ignorance among the people in the West about life in the Soviet Union and indeed the staggering lack of knowledge among the Russians of conditions in the free world.

It is surprising how many in the West, including Britain, still seem to believe that an average Russian usually wears a fur hat, a shirt hanging out and belted at the waist, and a flowing beard. During my lectures to Women's Institutes in the suburbs of London I frequently came across comments from my audience which implied that many of the ladies believed Russia was a rural country peopled largely by illiterate peasants. Many of them seemed quite unaware of the nature of the political system in Russia. 'Have they free elections in the Soviet Union, and which party is now in power?' was a question put to me a few years ago by a middle-class woman in Romford. The astonishing notions about the West one frequently comes across in Russia will seem less striking when one recalls that ignorance is by no means on one side only.

Most of the ordinary people in Britain are of course not deeply interested in the Russian way of life, but this is not the case with people in Russia, who are exceedingly keen to know how people live in the outside world. But even those who *are* interested in Soviet ways often jump to unwarranted conclusions as they fail to discriminate properly between what is typical and general and what is exceptional.

Contrasts in the Russian scene remain baffling. Tremendous progress, not only in space research but in many other fields, in medicine and other sciences, in education and literacy, can be seen side by side with extreme backwardness, neglect and muddle. One understands how this can happen; it is only possible in a country where the rulers are responsible to no one except to themselves and have virtually unchallenged command over human labour and resources so that these can be diverted to whatever purpose the dictators deem fit.

But even if one appreciates the arbitrariness of Russian leaders and the uneven nature of development one is still faced with a vast variety of contrasts and contradictions which defy rational explanation.

Then again, although it may now be easier to visit Russia than it was in Stalin's time, it is still very difficult to see much of the country and to learn the truth when talking to people. The USSR is still probably the most inaccessible and tightly supervised country in the world. Nowhere have I been shadowed more closely by the Security Police than in the Soviet Union. Nowhere have I had my luggage searched more thoroughly—usually when I was not present. Nowhere have I been approached by so many 'agents provocateurs', suggesting black market deals or offering sexual orgies as during my travels in the Soviet Union.*

*   *   *

From the outset severe limitations are placed in the way of a prospective visitor to the Soviet Union. Travelling in a group means being watched much of the time by the official guide and moreover such tours stop only a day or two in any one place as a rule, which makes it difficult to get to know the

* The Soviet Security Police seem to have a curious notion that all suspicious Westerners are sexually debauched. But in recent years the KGB has been particularly anxious to apprehend some 'James Bond' from Britain so that he could be conveniently exchanged for one of a number of Russian spies now lingering in British jails. Eventually, a British subject, Mr Gerald Brooke, was arrested and jailed in 1965. Yet the Russian authorities made a mistake if they believed, as they apparently did, that his work on behalf of a Russian *émigré* organisation was connected with the British Intelligence Service.

town well and make friends locally. Until very recently individual travel could only be done in the de-luxe class, costing twelve guineas a day all-in. Now tourist class travel at £5 a day is available. In any case, however, only a limited number of Soviet towns may be visited, although this has now been increased to 57. Most of the Russian provincial towns and villages remain closed to a Western tourist.

When in Russia one is constantly subjected to propaganda and indoctrination, often done in crude ways. The official guides are mostly young girls from universities and they are as a rule friendly and co-operative. I have seen books written by Western visitors about life in the Soviet Union based largely on information supplied by Intourist guides. I frequently witnessed Western visitors arguing themselves red-faced about some political point with a Russian guide. Yet these women, many of whom are quite pretty, are neither good-time girls (as some tourists seem to think) nor potential converts to anti-communism. They are there to do a job, which includes praising to the sky everything Russian.

When I was in Odessa, in 1961, the town was very short of fresh meat. I asked my guide, Sonia, a young teacher of English, what the meat situation was. She said that the shops were well stocked with it and that she and her family ate it every day. The price was about 5s. for a pound of beef. But when I asked for meat in one of the shops the assistant was astonished. 'Don't you know that State shops in Odessa have had no meat all this summer?', he said. He suggested that I should try the private market where peasants were selling produce at free prices. At 7 o'clock in the morning I found a long queue of people outside a shed in which very inferior beef was sold at about 10s. a lb. Other farm produce was on sale too, most of it at double the official prices.

Everybody in the Soviet Union lives under a blanket of political propaganda. Portraits of Lenin have now replaced the pictures of Stalin, equally ubiquitous in the past. The canny smile of the father of Russian communism may greet you in most unlikely places, with captions such as: 'Don't worry. You are taking the right road'. Slogans and exhortations accompany a Soviet citizen from cradle to grave. Among the least pleasant manifestations of propaganda is Russian radio, which blares out over amplifiers in streets and other public places—not so public ones too. I was jerked out of bed in an hotel in Minsk by the sound of the Soviet anthem very early in the morning. I toned down the volume of the receiver, but I could not switch it off entirely. To do that I would have had to tear out the wire.

If it is not easy for a foreign visitor to find his way to the truth in Russia how much more difficult it must be for a Russian—in Russia—to get a correct idea of the West. And even for the very few Russians who can travel to any Western country it is not easy. Although their number has been gradually increasing, they are still closely watched by their compatriots. When travelling as tourists they are in the care of their official guides who miss no opportunity of pointing to negative features of the country being visited. A young woman in Volgograd, herself an Intourist guide now, told me during my recent visit to the town that she had been to London. She said she particularly remembered 'the appalling sight of an old woman in tatters selling matches'. 'Have you no social services in England?', she asked.

A Russian fellow passenger in a train once asked me what a pair of shoes cost in England and how many pairs an average industrial worker could buy with his monthly pay (in Russia he can buy about three pairs). When I told him, he said: 'You take me for a fool', and refused to talk to me any further. I conversed with a student in a park in Kiev. He was preparing for his finals in economics. 'Does your Army shoot at workers when they strike?', he asked.

None the less, there are ways by which a Russian citizen can learn about life in the West. Specially important as a source of information are Western short-wave broadcasts in the Russian language, such as those of the BBC, the Voice of America and Radio Liberty (an American station operating from

Munich). I found that the BBC was particularly widely regarded as a reliable source of prompt and objective information. Jamming of BBC broadcasts in Russian has now ceased, making it possible to include a greater variety of programmes with more sophisticated discussions and music.

Listening to such programmes is now quite common in Russia, partly because the younger generation particularly are keenly interested in intellectual matter of all kinds, due perhaps to the exceptional emphasis in Russia on formal education and a generally serious tone of life. Listening to Western broadcasts is, however, not regarded as a habit worthy of a good Party member. 'I don't listen myself,' a 21-year-old member of the communist youth organisation, the Komsomol, said to me. 'But some of my friends like to listen to jazz music.' But it later became clear from my discussions with him that he followed BBC programmes fairly closely.

Foreign newspapers can be a significant source of information in the main cities and towns. Only those with communist views are generally available to the public, but the people who can read Serbo-Croat or Polish may be able to learn a good deal more about the outside world than if they were confined to the Soviet press. The London *Daily Worker** is widely available in the Soviet Union and assumes a special significance. 'I don't know English, but I look at the pictures,' said a man who regularly took the paper. 'I can see how people are dressed. I can see in other ways too that life is really far better in England than our government would like us to think.'

Soviet authorities go to great lengths in their attempts to distort the picture of life in the free world. Reporting on events in Britain, the USA and other Western countries in Soviet newspapers is calculated to bring out unfavourable features. In a boarding school in Volgograd in 1964 I thumbed through the cuttings that are stuck on the wall every morning for the pupils to read when passing by. Without exception the items reflected crude anti-Western propaganda.

An American member of our group asked a boy of ten in

* Now *The Morning Star*

the school if he would like to visit the USA. 'No,' the boy replied, 'I will never wish to go there. There are too many slaves in America.'

Yet in this same school our group of tourists, numbering ten people of no particular significance, was received with overwhelming hospitality. The headmaster and his entire staff received us in the friendliest way, a ballet performance in which about a hundred girls took part was laid on for us, we were shown around classes and dormitories, and everywhere we went little boys with red scarves stood as a kind of guard of honour. As we left the whole school assembled in the court-yard to pay their farewells while the boys' brass band played and girls' choir sang. Bouquets were presented to women members of our group. Similar receptions took place in other establishments we visited under the auspices of the Soviet national tourist agency.

Talking to Russian people is no longer a problem. They are no longer afraid to talk to foreigners—but they are still afraid of telling the truth. However, anyone coming from the West with the knowledge of the language is instantly bombarded with such typical questions as: 'How much unemployment is there in England? How do workers live? Are schools expensive? Why do you rearm Germany?'

Any information thus received will be set against the official line which the Russian is given by his government. And who is telling the truth? The Russian too is often baffled. Besides, there are many things which are difficult to grasp for a man brought up in an entirely different society. Talking to a factory manager in southern Russia I was asked the following characteristic question:

'Your businesses are, as you say, largely owned by private individuals and are motivated by the pursuit of profit. Each unit looks after its own success. How can you then fulfil your national plan?'

'We have no national plan.'

'But how then can the needs of the people be met—the

needs of industry—and the State itself? How can economic progress be achieved on a national scale?'

Another topic which both fascinates a Soviet citizen and eludes his comprehension is the position of the Queen.

'Suppose the heir-apparent is a person of low ability. Yet he, or she, will none the less succeed to the throne when the monarch dies.' That was a remark made to me by an educated Russian. That a sovereign in Britain reigns but does not rule is incomprehensible to an average Russian whose ideas of a non-communist system are still largely derived from what he knows, or has been told, about Czarist Russia.

Being himself largely ignorant of the West, the Russian normally assumes that a Western visitor knows little about him. This explains perhaps why a Russian guide never hesitates to assure you that what you have just seen with her was not a showpiece of some kind but a typical example of the most ordinary kind in Russia.

In 1964 I was taken round a coal mine in the Donets Basin. 'Just a typical Soviet coal mine,' my guide explained. Coal cutting was automatic. Transport underground, ventilation and safety arrangements were of the highest standard. There was a registered full-time nurse in charge of a small casualty bay underground. She apparently knew of my arrival, because when I entered the room she had two bundles of bandages ready for me on her table, to give as a present. Coal miners here claimed to be earning about £160 a month—over three times the average salary of a doctor in Russia. They had one month's paid holiday every year, which they said they could spend in a sanatorium or rest home, partly or wholly at the expense of the community.

These were in fact real coal miners, but not representative. They were exceptionally lucky to work in such an establishment and to be treated so well, but this was *not* typical of what I saw elsewhere.

The coal mine was, in fact, just as untypical as a State farm I visited near Kiev. Here tomatoes and cucumbers were produced in hothouse conditions by most imaginative and scientific methods. The manager insisted that this was a more economic way of growing vegetables than in the open. But in Kiev itself one could buy no tomatoes, and only occasionally rather inferior cucumbers.

Many of the Western tourists who take conducted tour trips to Russia under the auspices of Intourist hope to be able to see a Soviet farm. This is a most frequent subject of arguments and discord between the Russian guide and the visitors. Before they left New York or London or wherever they came from the tourists had been promised a visit to a Soviet farm when they booked their tour. Why couldn't they see one? If persistent, or able to pull some strings in the right place, the tourist may be shown a farm. But it is usually of the kind just described. In 1961, when I was touring the Ukraine as an individual tourist, I was taken to a farm near Odessa. 'Unfortunately', my guide said, 'we cannot see any farmers. They all work in the fields. And we cannot visit their homes, because they are out. But we can see their club. It is just a typical club for farmers in the Soviet Union.'

The club had a theatre hall for 800 people, with marble pillars and golden chandeliers and upholstered chairs. Adjacent to it was a large library. Another large room was filled with pianos, trumpets and violins. 'This is for our collective farmers to practise music when they return from work,' my guide explained.

Such marvels are, of course, not there just to impress a foreign visitor. Like the celebrated Moscow underground, with its ornate magnificence, they are a kind of pointers to the future, something to keep up the spirit of the Russian people. I talked to a young student in a park in Odessa about the 'farmers' club'. 'Oh, yes,' she said. 'I saw it too. All our school was once taken there. Children come to see it from as far away as a hundred miles.' Like many things Russian, such showpieces have a quasi-religious quality. When travelling in the Moscow Metro one is indeed curiously reminded of a place of worship, perhaps because of the hushed silence, the ban on smoking, the mosaics on the walls and the corpulent, kerchiefed women scrubbing the floors on their knees.

There is also a strange notion of Soviet communist leaders that Russian workers and peasants should ultimately be able to live in a way resembling as closely as possible the life of the upper middle classes just before the Revolution. This explains, perhaps, the odd obsession with potted plants, gilded mirror frames and red plush furnishings so often to be seen in the Soviet Union.

Another example of this sort of thing are the 'sanatoria' in Sochi and elsewhere. A Russian friend whom I met in Sochi in 1964 insisted, after a couple of vodkas, on taking me to see his 'sanatorium', the 'Metallurg'. 'You can see how our workers are able to spend their holidays,' my host said as we made our way through lush tropical vegetation, past rustic ponds and fountains. An enormous staircase, lit by ornate lamps, led up to giant pillars flanking the entrance to the sanatorium. The interior was like a palace turned into a museum; guests were moving about in awed silence. My friend was a middle-aged engineer from Siberia. It was his first time in Sochi, and very likely his last. There was nothing particularly wrong with his health, but he was clearly given this holiday for some exceptional services.

In Kiev I talked to a family by the river Dnieper one hot summer day. The sandy beach was covered with bodies, most of them oversize. Across the huge, darkish river was the capital of the Ukraine, nestling in the green of its hills and parks, with the golden cupolas of the Petcherskaya Lavra monastery gleaming in the sun.

'Have you had your holiday yet?', I asked the wife.

'This *is* our holiday,' she said. 'We come here every day, my husband and the children. The fare is only a few kopeks from where we live.'

'But don't you want to go to the Crimea?'

'I would love to,' she said, 'but I can't afford it.'

'What about your trade union or some other organisation? Will they not pay?'

In reply, she laughed broadly (showing two steel crowns in

her front teeth). What she meant was that to people of her kind, to most of the ordinary people in Russia, State or Trade Union-assisted holidays on the Black Sea are something in the nature of winning a thousand roubles on the lottery, something that practically never happens.

Most of the Russian people one sees in such places as Yalta or Sochi come there at their own expense, living in grossly overcrowded flats and paying about £2 a day for food and lodging. To have spent a holiday on the Black Sea carries unusual social prestige in the Soviet Union. Yet it is a measure of the growing prosperity of the Soviet people that (however low the proportion of the population) more and more of them do in fact spend their holidays on the Black Sea. In Sochi, which is a lovely seaside resort at the foothills of the magnificent Caucasus mountains, the number of visitors in 1964 was three times what it was five years before.

In such seaside resorts one finds people from all over the Soviet Union and from all walks of life. It is easier here than anywhere else to make friends and talk freely, as most people are strangers to each other. It was during my visits to Yalta in 1961 and Sochi in 1964 that I gained a fresh insight into the thinking of a section of the Soviet people who are most elusive and difficult to assess statistically: the anti-communists.

A young professional woman whom I had met through a friend told me she felt actual physical pain when looking at symbols of communist rule. We were walking about in Gurzuf, a small town near Yalta, consisting mostly of quaint old houses with delicate wooden balconies in which Tartars had lived before they were deported after the last war. A detachment of red-scarved 'pioneers'—young boys' organisation—marched by, bawling martial songs. I asked how she came to hate so much the régime under which she had been living all her life. She said her father brought her up in this way. Yet he was himself a high-ranking Party official.

A 35-year-old scientist from Leningrad on holiday in Yalta said threequarters of what he described as 'thinking people'

73

in the Soviet Union were opposed to the régime. But, he added, people were used to living a double life, thinking one thing and saying another. We turned our heads every now and again for fear of being overheard as we walked through a wooded park skirting the town and then up a hill overlooking the pretty bay. It was impossible to find a place where one could be absolutely assured of privacy, for at six in the morning Yalta and the surrounding country were already teeming with holidaymakers and the rocky beach was packed with people (including large Soviet women sunbathing in their underwear).

'My only hope', my Russian friend said, 'is to leave this country and go to the West.' Could I help him? I said I had heard in Odessa that sailors of foreign ships, especially of Arab nations, were occasionally prepared to take refugees on board—at the cost of about £200 (in roubles) and grave peril of being discovered by Soviet guards. (The only other way to escape is to leave officially with a travelling group, and then defect—but that is difficult and dangerous too.)

My friend's main complaint about life in the Soviet Union was that the people had no control over a government which was entirely arbitrary and unpredictable in its decisions.

One could write at length about Russia from what one heard when talking to confirmed anti-communists. That one can meet a great many such people in the Soviet Union is in itself significant. But any organised, articulate opposition to the régime is promptly suppressed. Life may be freer now than it was under Stalin when a single denunciation was sufficient to send one to a concentration camp or death. It needs now, as my scientist friend in Yalta explained, the testimony of at least two people to send one to prison for anti-communist views and activities. But the Russian Security Police, the KGB, remains ubiquitous and powerful.

Yet, interesting though the Russian anti-communists are, they are not always reliable sources of information. In Sochi I became friendly with a former Army officer and war hero who was now employed as a garage mechanic, earning £40 a month. He took me to his home which consisted of a tiny

74

room in which his wife and three daughters lived. The only toilet was in the courtyard of the old ramshackle building, inhabited by a large number of people.

'I have been waiting for a decent flat since 1947,' he said. His picture of Russia was one of utter gloom, and he insisted that I should share his view.

The opinions voiced by anti-communists in Russia provide one of the striking contrasts of the Soviet scene when they are compared with the statements of official guides, or for that matter of patriotic Soviet citizens, of whom there are plenty.

There are many other contrasts; for example, the difference between life in Moscow and the two other leading cities, Kiev and Leningrad, on the one hand, and provincial towns on the other.

On leaving Moscow in 1964 for a tour of the provinces I was told by a Russian friend at Vnukovo airport, 'You won't find any white bread once you are out there.' His warning did not disturb me particularly. To my friend, as indeed to many Russians, white bread is, however, a staple diet and a mark of progress on earlier times. But 1964 was bad for white bread in the Soviet Union. Only the three leading cities were adequately supplied with it. This was one instance of the gap which separates the big cities from the rest of the country.

Although drab by Western standards, life in Moscow or Leningrad appears gay and attractive to the inhabitants of Soviet provincial towns. The best theatres and artists are in the leading cities. In the sphere of culture Moscow and Leningrad provide a kind of window to the outside world, and it is here too that the old Russian heritage, whatever is left of it, mainly survives.

One reason for the differences in standards lies in the enormous distances separating towns in Russia. Only air travel will alter this. I thought of this as the Tupolev jet bore me, comfortably and at high speed, towards a distant city in the South. The passengers aboard the plane looked as if they might have been travelling on a bus in an English industrial town. Women with babies in their laps were wiping sweat from their brows. Men in shirt sleeves, without ties, and wearing soft caps or hideous straw hats, looked as though they had just clocked out of their factories. Air travel is taken as a matter of course by many Russians. From Moscow to Rostov-on-Don takes only two hours by air, compared to 19 by train, and costs less. A Czech visitor told me he had sold a pair of his old shoes in Kiev and bought a jet plane ticket to the Crimea with the money.

No doubt if progress in aviation goes on at the present pace a time will come when differences between the leading centres and provincial towns will shrink. But at the moment they still provide some of the bewildering contrasts in which the Russian scene abounds.

'I shall do everything I can to move to Moscow,' an acquaintance said to me in Rostov-on-Don. 'I don't wish my children to grow up here.' In Moscow, he explained, his children would get a better education and their chances of making a career would be much greater. Yet there seemed to be no shortage of educational establishments in Rostov-on-Don, or for that matter in any of the other provincial towns I visited. My Intourist guide informed me that there were no less than 100 secondary schools, 42 colleges and institutes, one university, 22 research institutes, 122 medical establishments, four 'live' theatres and 42 cinemas, all in a town of about 700,000 people. The fact is, however, that the quality of teaching tends to be much superior in Moscow, and a degree of Moscow University carries unsurpassed prestige in the USSR.

But the problem faced by the people like my friend in Rostov is how to obtain permission to settle in Moscow. This depends not only on the work one does but also on whether one can find living accommodation in the capital. Actually, permission to move to Moscow is given only in exceptional cases. But ways are sometimes found. For example, I was told that a single person (of either sex) will arrange a marriage with a partner already living in Moscow; then, once the spouse is safely established there, the couple obtain a divorce that had been agreed in advance.

Most of the provincial towns are closed to foreign visitors. But whenever I could I availed myself of the opportunity to taste the forbidden fruit, when my aeroplane was diverted, or the train stopped for some reason or other for a couple of hours in an out-of-the-way place. What I saw was always interesting as, after all, the bulk of the Soviet people live in provincial towns and villages.

I have a particularly vivid recollection of a visit I paid one day to Byelaya Tserkov, a town about 70 miles from Kiev. Having arranged a 'day off' with the Intourist guide at my hotel I simply joined a rather long queue very early in the morning at one of Kiev's coach stations. I had no trouble whatever in getting to my destination and back in the same day.

What I saw in Byelaya Tserkov reminded me sharply of wartime German propaganda pictures of the Soviet Union. Thick clouds of dust enveloped the roads, which were pitted in places with holes a foot deep and more. Barefooted girls were carrying buckets of water from a well. In a stagnant pool middle-aged women were splashing about in the summer heat, naked but for their black cotton pants. A man who sat down next to me told me he had not been paid any wages for the past two months. 'This happens quite frequently,' he said. 'The trouble is, out here we are far away from the main office of the enterprise.' He was a construction worker, he told me, and had a sick wife and two children to support.

A desecrated Catholic church, now little more than a ruin, was the chief landmark of this depressing town which largely consisted of wooden bungalows. I could see only one shop in the entire town, and the goods on sale were inferior to, and more expensive than, similar items in Kiev shops. 'Shops in main towns often get permission from central authorities to lower their prices when certain of their products are a bit sticky,' a shop assistant told me, adding, 'We never have any difficulty in selling anything.'

Only recently the Soviet leaders have begun to pay attention to the tragedy of small, provincial towns which have been by-passed by Stalin's industrial revolution and their former industries and crafts left to decay, causing much unemployment. Many of these formerly prosperous towns have been reduced to large villages, lacking such amenities as canalisation, piped water and gas.

Owing to lack of employment locally and inability to find accommodation in towns many people in Russia travel long distances daily to work in urban centres, often for exceedingly low wages. A 21-year-old girl digging ditches with a pick in a Kiev park told me she travelled 26 miles each way daily, earned just over £14 a month and worked a 41-hour week.

While most of the essential consumer goods now seem to be available in cities like Moscow or Leningrad—and in this respect there has been a marked improvement in both variety and quality of products over recent years, to some extent because of imports from eastern Europe—the situation is radically different in the provinces. People in Rostov told me they could not buy electric wire or bulbs and a great many other articles of daily necessity. To purchase such items they must either travel to Kiev or Moscow, or ask someone else to do it for them.

In Volgograd, a Russian teacher friend asked me to sell him a pair of nylon socks, for which he offered me just over £1. I thought he wanted them because synthetic textiles are as yet exceedingly rare in the Soviet Union. 'No,' he said, 'I simply cannot get a pair of socks in town, not even cotton or woollen ones.' He said he occasionally travelled to Leningrad, where he had relatives, to buy things that he could not obtain locally —for example, spare parts for an old motor-car that he had parked in his garden. He would re-sell some of the purchases to his friends at a small profit, thus supplementing his salary of just under £36 a month.

My friend was living with his wife and two children in a house of his own, situated in a private housing estate in a Volgograd suburb. 'I would much prefer to live in a council flat,' he told me, but after waiting in vain for some 15 years he had finally given up. 'Had I been a Party member,' he said, 'I would have had no difficulty.'

His house was a small, one-storey structure, with three rooms and a kitchen. There was electricity, and the family had radio and television sets. The estate contained some 300 houses of similar construction. 'None has an inside toilet,' my friend told me. Each house merely had a primitive lavatory standing in the backyard. Water had to be fetched from a pump up the road, which served some hundred families. My friend had paid about £1,600 for his house.

When I went out to his home I took a taxi. The driver stopped the car about half a mile from the estate and let me out, explaining that he could go no farther because the road was too bad. It was indeed. As I walked on in the direction he indicated I sank ankle deep in the mud every now and then. 'When there is heavy rain or snow,' my friend told me, 'the roads out here become practically impassable. Few people can even get to work.' Later, when I stepped out of my friend's house in the darkness to go back to my hotel, I fell into a ditch, sinking knee deep in mud. This was apparently not an unusual mishap.

From the house we walked about half a mile to the nearest bus stop and there we had to wait for about half an hour before the bus arrived. It was a 20-minute ride back to the centre of Volgograd, but the fare was only five kopeks.

Yet living in a provincial town like Volgograd, and more particularly in a suburban area such as where my friend had his home, is not without its advantages. One man on the estate said, 'Here we need have no fear of Party snoopers. Nobody here is a communist.' The man explained that in the last three years they had been called only twice to attend political gatherings and there was very little political pressure or chicanery of any kind, this in sharp contrast to the descriptions given to me by people who live in large blocks of flats in the main cities and have to attend political meetings regularly and frequently.

Volgograd was almost completely destroyed in the last war and its population practically vanished, but it now has about 680,000 inhabitants, compared with about 445,000 in 1939. Such increases of town populations are typical, for people are

79

leaving the land in search of better employment and a fuller life. The result is a tremendous housing problem in the towns.

Volgograd has now been almost completely rebuilt in a style that is largely dull and forbidding save for the well-arranged flower beds in the centre of the city and spacious avenues lined with trees. As a reminder of the ravages of the war, one solitary bombed-out building has been left standing and is now much photographed by foreign visitors, mainly delegations from other communist countries which arrive in the city almost daily. When I was there an enormous monument was being hewn out of rock on the spot where the fiercest fighting took place in the heroic defence of the city against the Germans.

Almost everywhere in the Soviet Union one can see evidence that the housing problem, which was virtually ignored for decades, is now being energetically tackled. Large blocks of flats, some of them approaching contemporary styles, with balconies painted in vivid red or blue or orange, are mushrooming on the outskirts of cities and towns. 'We build more houses per year than any other country,' boasted our guide in one of the places I visited in 1964.

Still, Soviet authorities admit that housing construction usually lags behind planned schedules. There appeared to be no shortage of unskilled labour for such construction projects, probably because of the large number of people moving into towns from rural areas and anxious to find any sort of work. Russia is, moreover, in a position apart with regard to its labour force, due to the unusually wide range of jobs for which women can be recruited. In the USSR nearly as many women as men are employed and female labour is used extensively in the building trade, performing even the heaviest work as bricklayers and navvies. It is clear, however, that both skilled labour and building materials are much more readily available in the main cities than in the provinces. In the more remote provincial towns one often sees construction workers using very primitive tools, and the workmanship is usually inferior.

Even in the main cities the quality of new housing construction still leaves much to be desired in spite of some improvement over the last few years. 'We are learning all the time,' said the building foreman who showed our group through some newly-completed flats in Kiev. But in some of the rooms, the paint was already peeling off the walls and there was other evidence of crude workmanship and poor materials.

But the main problem in provincial towns and villages is that of food supply. In Volgograd, for instance, although potatoes were on sale in the large and modern enclosed market on the day I saw it in June 1964, I was told that none of this first staple Russian diet had been available in the town for some time past. And, even now that the potatoes were on sale, at 2s. 10d. a lb., they were too expensive for many people such as old-age pensioners who must live on a monthly income of about £15. Other vegetables too were scarce and hardly any fruit at all was available, with the exception of small, rather inferior oranges selling at 3s. 2d. each! Eggs could be bought at 1s. 2d. each and women in spotlessly clean white overalls were selling milk at 1s. 7d. a pint and butter at nearly £1 8s. 10d. a lb. The only meat available was some inferior pork at just over 7s. a lb. This meat, I was told, came from animals that had to be slaughtered because there was nothing to feed them with.

Elsewhere in the town the same day I saw long queues of housewives—200 in one queue—waiting to buy sugar at just under 5s. a lb. All these prices were substantially higher than in 1961.

In some towns which I was unable to visit shortages were apparently even more acute. I was told, for instance, that certain towns, such as Tula, south of Moscow, experienced conditions of near starvation in 1964, with children suffering particularly from lack of milk.

Sometimes also failures in the distribution system cause local shortages of foods not generally in short supply. Thus, although there was no general shortage of fish in Rostov-on-

Don, I noticed a large number of housewives waiting outside a fishmonger's shop at seven in the morning.

'We live even worse now than under Stalin,' a man in Rostov-on-Don complained to me. 'This year is worse than last, and 1963 was worse than 1962,' he added. Surprising as this statement seemed, it was echoed by several other persons I encountered during my visit in 1964.

These chronic food shortages have been causing acute embarrassment to the Soviet leaders, particularly in view of Moscow's efforts to woo and impress the developing world. I recall the comment made to me by a young African student whom I met in a Moscow café. 'I am surprised the Russians believe their system suitable for us Africans and Asians,' he said. 'We need food and other necessities of life above all, but the Russians seem to have even less to eat than we do.' He had been visiting a number of provincial towns.

Khrushchev had the merit of recognising the disastrous food situation in the country and being quite frank about it. He made it plain that communism would not be able to go on attracting recruits in the world if it failed to deliver the goods. He thereupon set about trying to make Russia a truly prosperous country and in 1958 launched a plan which, by the time of its completion in 1965, was to raise Soviet output of food per head of population to exceed that of the USA!

*   *   *

When I first travelled to Russia in 1960 and our bus crossed the Polish-Soviet frontier at Brest and we took the straight, long, and somewhat bumpy motorway to Minsk, Smolensk and the Soviet capital, our Russian guide explained that this road was paved with bones of invaders. Both Hitler and Napoleon had hurled their armies along this avenue, only to be thrown back in blood and confusion. The beautiful church at Smolensk, which attracts thousands of worshippers every Sunday from far and wide, was built in the seventeenth century to celebrate the deliverance from another invader, the Poles.

But now the Soviet authorities were above all concerned

that those travelling on this historic road should take in the good message of forthcoming prosperity. Large, freshly painted hoardings on both sides of the motorway told of the increase of output of milk, butter, meat and other products in the current seven-year plan. Effigies of Lenin and of young boys and girls, pointed with outstretched hands into the air, into the bright future.

Yet behind this carnival of propaganda one could see something of the Russian rural reality. Multitudes of women were kneeling on the ground, pulling up root crops; tired men in their heavy boots were returning to their homes on village tracks, carrying large sacks on their backs. Farmers' houses were small and primitive, if charming, with their traditional woodwork and white or blue painted walls. But this impression of bucolic backwardness was not universal. During a subsequent visit to some of the most fertile regions of the Soviet Union, in the South, I drove for hours past well-tended fields on which huge machines were operating, and all seemed very rational and advanced.

It is not quite easy to understand why there should be these shortages of food in Russia. Many people I talked to attributed them to Soviet aid abroad. But this aid represents only a relatively small proportion of Russia's total output. There are vagaries of the weather, of course. But as a man in the 'black earth' region of southern Russia said to me, 'We ought to be able to have enough to eat here, no matter what the weather is like'.

One of the reasons given to me by an angry housewife standing in a queue in Kiev waiting to buy butter was: 'Our peasants will not work for nothing. That's why we are short of food.'

Most of the *kolkhoz* peasants I met in Russia, on their farms and villages, or at railway or coach stations where they sit about with large sacks containing no one knows what, told me they were earning between 7 and 10 roubles a month—or £2 16s. to £4 at the official rate of exchange. In addition, they said, they were given produce daily—2 lb. of potatoes perhaps, or 1 lb. of wheat and a few other products of similar value. This was provided they had done their work on the collective farm. Men and women from State, or *sovkhoz*, farms seemed to be earning about £8 a month with no additional benefits.

Recently there have been some improvements in the life of Soviet farmers. Earnings have been increased somewhat and a compulsory minimum pension has been introduced for *kolkhoz* workers of £4 16s. a month. The Government has been paying out pensions when collective farms themselves were not able to afford them. But there is no certainty that such improvements have been universally applied in the USSR or that they have changed the situation very markedly. The material position of the Russian farmers did not seem to be much better in 1964 as compared to 1961 and the latest changes too have not altered the picture much, according to close observers.

By and large the Soviet farming folk, constituting at least one-third of the population, continue to live in misery. And agricultural output in the Soviet Union shows no real signs of improvement. In 1965 the harvest again was poor, inferior to that of 1964 although not as disastrous as that of 1963. The yields of crops in the USSR are lower than in any other communist country in Europe and very much lower than in the West,* although capital investment in Soviet farming has been substantially increased in recent years. In 1965 Russia placed orders in the West totalling a record amount of 9 million tons of wheat.

There is a striking contrast between the earnings of a farm worker and a man employed in town, hence the continuing pressure of rural people to move into urban centres in spite of the fact that it is illegal for a member of a collective farm to travel without a specific document authorising the journey.

When at home the Soviet *kolkhoz* peasants tend to concentrate their energies on the small plot they are allowed to have.

---

* The average yield of wheat in the good year of 1964 was less than 11 centners per hectare as compared to over 10 centners in pre-revolutionary Russia and 30–50 centners in western Europe.

As a rule this is not larger than one-quarter of a hectare—or just over half an acre—but it is not uncommon now to find private plots as large as one hectare. It is now also possible to keep any number of animals privately. These may be regarded as the most significant changes affecting Russian agriculture after the fall of Khrushchev. It has been estimated that even before these changes the tiny plots, constituting about 1 per cent of the total arable land, provided no less than one-quarter of the food consumed in the Soviet Union.

It remains to be seen now what further concessions to common sense the Soviet leaders will be prepared to make. The entire system of agriculture in Russia has been undergoing a process of agonising reappraisal.

Lack of proper incentives is not confined to agriculture. The entire system of production and distribution suffers from a chronic lack of balance between talent and productive effort on the one hand and reward on the other. Much is being built that is of no use to anyone. Many projects are started, then stopped for years when half finished, or less. Bureaucratic muddle, waste of resources and inefficient management assume gigantic proportions. Often this is admitted by Soviet leaders themselves when they indulge in 'self-criticism' and prepare the ground for changes.

There is a vast disproportion between the money that is available to buy goods in Russia and the amount of products people can or wish to buy.

One has no difficulty in seeing that the Soviet economy suffers from serious inflation, although outward symptoms may be suppressed. That there should be so much money about in Russia may come as a surprise. After all, salaries and wages are very low compared to prices. Most people I talked to in towns were earning about £40 a month, but many had to live on as little as £12 a month. Yet one could see large crowds of people in Russian shops buying all manner of useless trash (although it is also true that the accumulation of unsaleable goods has caused serious problems in some localities).

Restaurants and places of entertainment are usually filled

to capacity. Most significant is the apparent readiness of Soviet citizens to disburse quite large amounts of cash, on the spot, for Western clothing, footwear and other articles. I saw Western visitors selling in the streets of Russian towns old nylon shirts at £6 each, shoes at £8, flannel trousers at £20, and so on. Customers were often ordinary passers-by who considered the purchases a good buy.

There are, of course, many in Russia who buy foreign-made goods in order to resell them. Sentences passed on such people when caught are savage and increasing in severity. Yet I have not the slightest doubt that such trade continues on a large scale.

In Odessa I had a rare opportunity of making friends with quite substantial black marketeers who told me of their activities, which covered an area of several thousand miles. All manner of goods are traded in this way, anything that cannot easily be bought in shops. Gold and foreign currency were passing hands with a particularly high margin of profit, and the prices paid were in themselves a measure of the real value of the rouble in the eyes of the people. In Odessa in 1961 the black market rate for a pound note was five times the official rate.

It is a real tragedy for Russia that such genuine business acumen and effort should be driven underground. A black market friend said to me, 'We would create an economic miracle in Russia in six months time if we were allowed to trade freely.' Economically, one of the most negative aspects of illicit trade is that profits from it are never invested in a productive venture; they are spent on consumption, or turned into hard currency and gold, and hoarded.

There is no sign whatsoever that the Soviet Government is willing to allow any larger scope for private enterprise. Any concessions here would be regarded by many communists as a retrograde step, as the country is supposed to be moving rapidly to its final stage of development, according to Marxism-Leninism—that is, to the phase of 'communism' proper in which all people have their needs satisfied regardless of what they contribute to society.

Even the smallest private commerce is frowned upon, unless it be specifically tolerated, e.g. the private market of *kolkhoz* peasants and other independent producers of food. During my visit to Moscow in 1964 I saw at a street corner a selection of photographs and notices on a board. They referred to hooligans, drunkards and other social undesirables caught in the district recently. Names were given in full together with a detailed description of their misdeeds. On this board was also a photograph of an elderly woman selling flowers in a street. She too was publicly branded for trying to live 'an easy life by illicit trade'.

However, much of the State-run business too is based on extra-legal activities. State enterprises often rely on underhand suppliers for essential materials which they cannot get elsewhere in their efforts to fulfil the plan. It is believed that without such expedients it would be virtually impossible to carry on the Russian planned economy. Widely known in the Soviet Union, this system of 'Blat' accounts for a very large proportion of the total turnover of goods.

It has been obvious now for some time to many leading people in the Soviet Union that the present system of economy is in need of radical reforms. The system, which is still basically the same as it was under Stalin, may be very suitable for large concentrations of economic factors at selected points. Heavy industry has continued to make spectacular progress. But the system has failed to provide the people with what they really need and want. And this is now proving a far greater problem than in the time of Stalin when economic incentives could be ignored and concentration camps and outright death provided powerful deterrents for slackness or open discontent. Such instruments of compulsion are no longer available. Even in Russia consumers are gradually becoming a force that must be taken into account by the authorities.

* * *

In recent years the pages of Soviet journals and newspapers have been open to a lively debate on what should be done about the economic system. Needless to say, all suggestions must be argued strictly on the basis of Marxism-Leninism. None the less some of the proposals have been far-reaching and, if carried out, would move Russia close to a kind of 'socialist market economy'.

It is not surprising that such radical proposals have not been accepted, or at any rate not yet. One important obstacle to any really free interplay of supply and demand is the arbitrary and irrational nature of Soviet prices. But it is very difficult in a country like the USSR to effect any large changes, because of the vastness of the territory and the huge numbers of people who have been trained and conditioned to accept and work in the old ways. The enormous bureaucratic apparatus on which the Soviet State is based constitutes a powerful in-built conservative force in Soviet society. Moreover, Russia with her world-wide commitments and ambitions must be extremely reluctant to try such revolutionary experiments as have been carried out in Yugoslavia with uncertain prospects of success. Russia simply cannot afford a disastrous failure of a radical economic reform.

It is therefore not surprising if the new measures of reform announced by the Kosygin-Brezhnev régime fall far short of what some had expected, and indeed are far more timid than those introduced, or foreshadowed, in eastern Europe. But it is interesting that the Russians now seem to be following in the footsteps of their eastern European satellites, rather than the other way round.

There is, broadly, a common denominator between the Russian measures and the reforms in eastern Europe. Stemming from the same disillusionment with the Stalinist system, the reformers now seek to place more emphasis on the actual utility of products than on sheer quantity. Enterprises in Russia are given more powers of decision, although the abolition of regional economic councils set up by Khrushchev has meant a strengthening of central planning and administrative authorities in national terms. Profit is now given pride of place as an indicator of efficiency, whereas it was previously only a subordinate factor. The success of a business venture will depend on the actual sales rather than sheer output of goods.

There is, however, to be no freedom for prices to move according to the supply and demand in the market, such as has been allowed in Yugoslavia and to a smaller degree in Czechoslovakia. The 'Gosplan' still dominates the Russian economic scene. The planners in Moscow will continue to cater for most of the needs of enterprises and consumers.

4

Cinderella in the Tropics

Cuba

'YOU CANNOT BUY American cigarettes or Scotch with Cuban *pesos*,' the purser of the East German ship *Karl Marxstadt* told a protesting Cuban passenger. 'You can only buy them with hard currency.' But the Cuban went on protesting. Apart from me, he was the only passenger on a ship carrying 30 buses—made by Leylands in Britain—to Havana in May 1965. He was a Cuban film actor returning from an engagement in Leipzig.

An officer of the East German crew said later, 'These Cubans, they always want something for nothing. Their economy is a shambles. Their money is worth nothing. An East German mark at least has *some* international value—you can change 3.5 of our marks for one West German mark in West Berlin'.

We could already see in front of us the long, uneven silhouette of the city of Havana, with its skyscrapers gleaming in the bluish mist. American broadcasts had for some time been obliterated by jamming. On my transistor set a Cuban radio station was now heard transmitting old-fashioned tunes, identifying itself at frequent intervals: 'This is Cuba, Free Territory of America.'

When the ship reached harbour, dark-skinned, slightly-built and heavily-armed men in green cotton uniforms jumped on board and went meticulously through the papers handed to them by the East German captain. 'They are terribly fussy,' the blond captain, a man in his late twenties, remarked to me.

I had no trouble getting into Cuba. As a British subject I did not even need a visa. But two days after my arrival I was called to the Security Police Headquarters in Havana and subjected to a thorough interrogation lasting several hours. It was carried out by a heavily-perspiring young man in civilian clothes. But for a huge revolver on his hip he looked like a slightly ageing student.

'Have you ever been in Cuba before? Have you ever written about Cuba. Has your brother? Your father? Your mother? Have you ever been a member of a political organisation? Have you been to any other socialist country recently? What do you think of socialism? Of the USA? Do you agree with the American blockade of Cuba?'

Eventually he rose, adjusted his belt and revolver, and shook my hand, smiling for the first time. 'You are welcome here in Cuba. You can go anywhere you like. Talk to anyone you like.''

About a month later, on the day of my departure, I saw him again at Havana airport as he entered the lounge reserved for overseas passengers. For a moment, a cold shudder went down my spine. But he was escorting two young Americans who were being deported back to the USA, via Bermuda. They travelled on the same plane with me. They had arrived in Cuba three months earlier, having been shipwrecked in a severe storm, and since then they had been languishing in various Cuban jails.

In Havana I stayed at Habana Libre, the former Hilton hotel. Apart from minor signs of neglect (the radio in my room did not work) the magnificent, 25-floor hotel with its spacious halls, decorative pools and fountains, discreet background music and luxurious air-conditioned rooms, still bore all the marks of ostentatious elegance. In the cool water of the hotel's private swimming pool parties of men, women and children from the USSR and eastern Europe were splashing about noisily. This, like other first-class hotels in the city, was largely reserved for guests from 'other socialist countries'. A local man could not easily have afforded the prices anyhow.

In the hotel's night club, busy and gay till the early hours of the morning, the bill for one person might easily come to about £15. Most Cubans I saw in Havana were earning less than £35 a month. The majority of the guests here and in other night spots and expensive restaurants were members of communist delegations or other privileged persons whose expenses were paid by the Cuban Government. There were also a fair number of young local women.

Some of the eastern guests were more equal than others. The Russians certainly towered above everyone else in influence. A Belgian scientist, who had been invited by the Cuban Government to give a series of lectures at the Havana University, became involved through no fault of his own (as he explained to me) in a personal argument with a Russian guest in his hotel. Without bothering to go into the details of the quarrel the hotel manager told the Belgian to leave the hotel at once.

Russian technical advisers live in large modern villas, with military guards posted outside. These honoured guests also have special shops at their disposal where they may buy at reduced prices goods which are sometimes unobtainable locally. (Cuban communists above a certain rank also enjoy similar privileges.) In a residential hotel reserved entirely for the Russians and other eastern Europeans a friend and I visited the shop on the ground floor. Mango fruit, which could not be bought in ordinary shops in Havana, was on sale in neat cellophane bags, as well as other food and beverages and consumer goods. 'Look,' my Cuban friend said, 'the Russians have toothpaste too. I used the last of mine two months ago.'

I could obtain no unanimous opinion from my Cuban friends on whether life was now better or slightly worse than it had been a year or two years ago. Whatever the difference, it was plainly not very great. I certainly could see appalling shortages of almost everything. The Government blames the American blockade, but it is more relevant to point to the economic dislocations that have resulted from Castro's own policies. While food and consumer goods are mostly rationed, the available supplies hardly cover the elementary needs of the population.

Canteens are available for certain categories of employees, especially in important Government establishments, but the great majority of the people have no such facilities. To supplement the meagre rations, food can be bought on the black market where meat, for example, costs five times the official price in May 1965, or else one can eat in restaurants where moderate meals cost between £1 10s. and £3. Certain things could be obtained freely and at reasonable cost—bread, for example, and, oddly enough, eggs. But milk was unobtainable except for children under three and people over 65. I found the food situation even worse in the provinces than in the capital. While the meat ration in Havana was 12 ounces a week per person, outside the city it was only four ounces.

'But look at that'—I pointed to a crowd of small children pouring into the street from an improvised school in a former shop in Santiago de Cuba. 'Yes,' my Cuban friend said. 'Certain good things have been done. But', he added, 'I have never been hungry before.'

Education and social services are the two fields in which Castro's régime is believed to have done most for the Cuban people since the Revolution in 1959.

Like other communists, the Cuban leaders have an obsession about the struggle against illiteracy. In a tobacco factory in Havana I saw work come to a standstill at 10 a.m. for two hours while employees were taught to read and write, and the more sophisticated learned political history and other subjects in which the achievements of the communist régime could usefully be extolled. I had little difficulty in seeing that most of the 'pupils' (many of them elderly women) were intensely bored by this exercise and angered because they had to do two extra hours of work in the evening, without pay, instead of going home to their families.

The communists in Cuba are finding it hard to convince the people that the present misery is all somehow to the good. Communism has never been really popular in Cuba, although the Communist Party has been active on the island for many years. Cuba is largely a land of naturally gay, intelligent and individualistic people, mainly Spanish by descent and tradition. Marxism-Leninism has never been as widely known in Cuba as in Europe. I walked with a 30-year-old professional man down one of the main boulevards in Havana. I stopped in front of a large picture of Marx. My companion did not know who the man was.

It is true that there has been a good deal of poverty in Cuba in the past, especially among peasants and landless labourers, side by side with ostentatious wealth. A Cuban official took me to a luxurious seaside establishment near Havana. 'Only members of a club of wealthy men were allowed to bathe here,' he explained. 'Now it's open to Cuban workers.' There were very few bathers, but the beach was truly magnificent with its white, soft sand, the palm trees in the background and the crystal-clear sea shading to green close to the land.

Such extremes of social difference were undoubtedly galling to many sincere humanitarians in Cuba. The close dependence on the United States no doubt gave rise to genuine grievances on the part of Cuban nationalists. (I was often told the story of the American marine who urinated on a national monument in Havana.) It is also true that there were far too many gambling houses and prostitutes in Cuba before 1959. There is no doubt that the previous régime of the dictator Batista was unpopular. When Castro and his men emerged victorious they were riding on a high wave of national enthusiasm. But the new leaders did not say they were bent on making Cuba communist and a Russian satellite.

Whatever may have been the troubles and grievances in the pre-communist age, Cuba enjoyed fairly high standards of economic well-being, education and other attributes of civilisation. With a national income *per capita* of 353 dollars in the period between 1956 and 1958 Cuba ranked fifth among the twenty Latin American countries, second in energy consumption, first in railways, second in the number of private cars and first in television sets per head of population.*

The plain fact is that the Cubans as a whole now live considerably worse than they did under the hated dictator Batista.

'And what about the prostitutes?' I asked a Cuban friend who was himself a determined anti-communist. 'This business too has been nationalised [*consolidado*]', he said. 'But it still prospers.' He took me to see an entire street given over to prostitution, save for occasional houses on which was written in large letters: 'Please pass by, families live here.'

'Besides,' my friend said, 'many of our girls now go to bed with strangers just for a meal.' Many women previously employed as models or as artistes in cabarets now had their employment opportunities drastically reduced and a large number of them turned to prostitution, I was told.

The main problem of the Cuban leaders now is how to build up a truly devoted cadre of followers who can be entrusted with the management of the country's affairs. It is with this in view, no doubt, that exceptional importance is given to *becados*, or scholarship holders. There are now some 140,000 of these boys and girls, mainly recruited from the poorest sections of the population, who are educated away from their homes. One could see truckloads of girls in light, pink blouses being taken from one place to another, no doubt to inspect some model farm or new industrial project. I saw them also in what used to be a fashionable district of Havana, the

* *The Cuban Revolution and Latin America* by Boris Goldenberg (George Allen and Unwin, London, 1965), p. 120.

Miramar, with their heads poking out in clusters from the windows of villas that had been taken over from the enemies of the Revolution.

Oddly enough, in many of the villas in this district also live families of men who had been sent to concentration camps for suspected collaboration with anti-Castro guerrillas. In a small room in one of these villas I saw one woman living with her 11 children. The place was not guarded, but the grown-ups were not allowed to leave the place. Children could move freely in the neighbourhood and could attend school. The families were given food and some clothing, but no money. Some had been in this condition for more than two years; others had arrived more recently. I was told there were some 50,000 such people who had been driven from their homes in the provinces of Las Villas and elsewhere, and their farms given to others.

At night one could still hear shooting in the mountains around Camagüey. I heard people say that armed opposition to the Castro régime was still active, but I am not inclined to attach too much importance to such reports, or for that matter to other speculations regarding an imminent uprising in Cuba. In no other communist country have I heard so much grumbling and seen so few people who were convinced communists as in Cuba. But I was equally aware of the presence of a very strong military and police force ready to crush instantly any sign of rebellion. Of course, the leaders of the loosely-knit ruling Party, the PURSC, may find themselves one day at each other's throats—which might change the entire situation.

I heard many rumours of disagreements among the top leaders. But Fidel Castro towers above all others in influence and prestige. He is still the man who matters most in Cuba. And he is comparatively popular, although far less so than in the past. He can speak the language of the downtrodden masses of the Cuban people, especially of the rural folk, the *campesinos*. He can still command genuine enthusiasm among substantial numbers of the population.

Yet any overt opposition is savagely suppressed and the prison population as estimated by my friends in Cuba was at least double the official figure of the 15,000 admitted by the authorities. At the time of my visit the number of prisoners in the notorious La Cabana in Havana (and there are many other jails in the city) was given to me as 2,264 by a man who had just been released.

I could see that the atmosphere of siege was studiously cultivated by the Government. Men and women volunteered to guard government buildings. To do such duties, and indeed to co-operate with other voluntary activities and campaigns, is to be on the right side of the fence with the authorities. Outside my hotel a pretty girl was sitting on a chair for many days in succession. She had her skirt pulled up well above the knees and nursed a heavy rifle absentmindedly, like an unwanted baby. 'We do days. Men do nights,' she told me.

'See that ship?' My official guide pointed to the sea. 'It's an American spy ship with electronic devices. It comes every day. We could sink it in a few seconds if we wanted to. We have our own missiles now,' he boasted.

We sped along a magnificent motorway in the breathtaking way official Cuban drivers always seem to do, to visit a State farm. We passed through green, hilly country on our left, where giant palms with their grey, slender trunks and bushy tops dotted the fields like extravagant decorations. I could see many gun emplacements with their long, thin barrels nervously probing the sky.

'Granja de Revolución,' in the province of Pinar del Río, was a model farm, well above the average no doubt. There were over 57,000 acres of land with a variety of crops and some 10,000 head of cattle, many of them recently imported from Canada. Russian and Rumanian tractors were throbbing on the fields and there were also Soviet technicians on the farm. I saw a well-equipped cowshed with modern milking devices and tanks originating from different parts of the world, mainly from communist countries. Yet milk yields were low at 11 pints a day on average from a cow.

96

Workers lived in small but pretty and comfortable bunga-lows. ('Unfortunately they are not used to modern hygiene,' my guide explained.) And the farm labourers I interviewed told me they were earning over £8 a week. This was an improvement on the past, they said, when they were often unemployed between seasons. But, as one said to me, 'I could then buy more with the money I earned than I can now.' The pair of cotton pants he was wearing, he said, had cost him just over £1 but now he would have to pay over £4 for them. I was surprised that even the poor landless farm workers had apparently not profited by the régime. Yet there could be no doubt that many such labourers had now found cushy jobs in the large State *latifundias* which dominated the farming scene in Cuba. Others had left the land in search of more congenial employment in towns. At all events, the shortage of manpower, especially at the time of sugar harvest, remains one of the greatest problems in Cuban economy.

Wisely, the Cuban leaders have reconsidered their priorities and now give farming precedence over industrial develop-ment. Sugar is again king, as it once was, and second in im-portance is cattle breeding for which the conditions are good in Cuba. But the more ambitious industrialisation programmes have been shelved, following some disastrous attempts and failures.

In a sense it can be said that Cuba is avoiding the mistakes made by other communist régimes. On the other hand, the Cuban leaders had very little choice. They lacked the means to carry out industrialisation programmes such as were attempted in eastern European countries. But they have certainly learned little from the failure of socialised agricul-ture in the rest of the communist world. They are not willing to offer even such incentives to the farmers as are now custo-mary in Russia and elsewhere in the communist world.

Most of the land has been allotted to large State farms in which the workers have no rights of self-government and the management itself has little to say in production and planning. All important decisions are made by government departments to fit in with a national farming plan. There are a small number of collective farms, based on the Russian *kolkhozes*, but their members have no right to private plots. Seventy per cent of the arable land is now in government ownership, the rest being left to private farmers who may own up to 67 hectares.

A small independent farmer in the fertile province of Güines, once regarded as the 'kitchen garden of Havana', explained to me that he was deriving a net income of just over £30 a month from his 50-acre farm. Before the Revolution, as a sharecropper on the same land, he was earning about £25, nominally. Now he was made to deliver all his market-able surplus to State agencies at low fixed prices. What he bought for himself and his family had increased in cost a great deal more than the increase of his nominal earnings. He employed a permanent farm labourer and paid him about £15, as against £12 a month in the past. But the labourer too said he was worse off than before. There were 20 cows, two oxen, one horse, four pigs and some poultry on the farm.

'We have made a mess of our agriculture,' a senior Cuban official told me frankly. It is obvious that production of many key commodities has declined disastrously. In a speech on 27 January 1965, in Havana, the then head of the Cuban organisation for agriculture, the INRA, Señor Carlos Rafael Rodriguez, admitted that yields in farming were generally very low in 1964. He also revealed that the output of some staple foods had decreased. For example, the output of sweet potatoes in 1964 was just under 2 million quintals as compared to 5 million in 1960 and nearly 4 million in 1959.

It is true that the sugar harvest in 1965 reached a high level at over 6 million tons, although this was less than in the best pre-revolutionary years. But this relative success in 1965 was due to an unprecedented mobilisation of outside labour for cane-cutting. I saw office clerks, teachers, film actors and others who had all done a spell of cane-cutting under the scorching sun and with an inadequate diet. 'I had to do it,' one said, 'but I did not like it.' Hundreds of thousands of men and women from the towns were engaged in harvesting, in addition to entire Army units. It is clear that productivity in sugar farming will have to be raised substantially if the government plan of a harvest of 10 million tons is to be met by 1970.*

Experiments have been made with mechanical cutting of cane, but so far these have been inconclusive. The Cuban soil does not lend itself easily to mechanised harvesting. The Soviet combine harvesters, which in 1965 operated for the first time on Cuban fields, proved a failure by almost universal consent. Five hundred of these combine harvesters, operated partly by teams of young Russian technicians, could not cut the cane successfully, except when the ground was even, which is rare in Cuba. They were large, clumsy and difficult to operate. Their lifting gear often picked up masses of earth and stones with the cane; they could only work in fine weather and in daytime. They were withdrawn in the latter part of May, well before the harvest was completed. A simpler machine a Czecho-Cuban invention, was being tested.

Besides, a projected output of 10 million tons of sugar would necessitate the investment of some 450 million *pesos* (about £160 million) in the sugar mills, whose equipment has greatly deteriorated, and in transport vehicles.

Yet sugar remains of key importance for Cuba. It provides some 90 per cent of all foreign currency earnings and the ultimate emancipation of Cuba hinges on the fortunes of the sugar industry. But communist critics of Cuban economy were right in the past when they stressed the uncertain nature of sugar as a foreign exchange earning commodity, considering the wide fluctuations of the product in world markets.

In 1965 the world market price of sugar had sunk to below 2 cents a pound whereas it was more than 11 cents in 1963. It is true that a major part of Cuban sugar output is earmarked, by long-term agreements, for other communist countries, at fixed prices of about 6 cents a pound. The Soviet Union herself has agreed to purchase Cuban sugar at such a price in growing proportions of the planned harvest. By 1970 Russia would buy 5 million tons of sugar from Cuba, or half the entire

* Sugar harvest in 1966 was substantially lower than in 1965.

99

planned output. But this apparent advantage has a wholly political motive as Russia does not in fact need Cuban sugar. The fulfilment of the agreement on Russia's part is, of course, as usual, subject to political agreement between the two countries. Moreover sugar commitments to the Soviet Union and other communist countries make Cuba in turn dependent on products coming from that part of the world. There are also reports that Russia charges Cuba higher prices than would be warranted by international standards.

Yet, by and large, Cuba is a financial burden to the USSR, to the tune of about a million dollars a day, according to well-informed sources. My Cuban friends estimated that the number of Russian civilians in Cuba might be 3,000 and there was an equal number of eastern Europeans. All of them were assumed by the local population to be 'Russos'.

The Russians I saw on the island—and they could be found in all parts of the country, in factories, on farms, in hospitals and elsewhere—seemed to be well above the average of their countrymen in appearance and intelligence. But their public image in Cuba (as well as that of their products) is well short of expectations.

'We have had very little experience of supplying equipment to a tropical country,' a Soviet engineer said when I talked to him at one of the top Russian projects in Cuba, the thermo-electrical plant at Mariel, some 35 miles from Havana. I was told that hundreds of Russian scientists and technicians had worked on the project, the ultimate capacity of which was to be about 500,000 kw. The scheme was one of the most advanced yet attempted by the Soviet Union in Cuba. The plant was to be automatically operated, with much of the electronic equipment, however, coming from Western companies. The start of the first unit had been scheduled for 26 July, the Cuban National Day. But a technician said, 'We shall be lucky if we are ready to start next November.' It appears that the Cubans have been profoundly disappointed with the quality of Soviet steel, ball-bearings, design and other aspects of the equipment for the Mariel plant.

I also heard criticism of Soviet lorries, thousands of which have been supplied to Cuba in recent years. Many of these vehicles are ex-Army stock and some had been passed on from the Aswan Dam project where they had been found unsuitable. 'They cost more to run than the value of the sugar cane they carry,' I was told by a Cuban driver. He added that when fully loaded the lorries consume a gallon of petrol every six kilometres. An engineer in Cuba told me he had seen Russian lorries piled up by the roadside, finished and useless less than a year after their arrival in Cuba.

At the new Cuban shipyard, the 'Victoria de Giron', where small trawlers are built, I heard complaints about Russian and Chinese steel which is used for ship-plates.

Not all products coming from the communist world are bad or deficient, of course. I heard that the new Soviet diesel locomotives for Cuban railways were tough and reliable. Besides, deliveries to Cuba often had to be made in a great hurry, to meet delivery dates which Western companies would consider impracticable. Then again, Russian and eastern European supplies of essentials, such as petrol, filled absolutely vital gaps.

Some of the eastern European goods *are* of international standard, e.g. Skoda cars, of which I saw a sprinkling in Havana and some other towns. I was also told that Rumanian tractors were tough and suitable for tropical conditions. Some of the consumer goods coming from eastern Europe are quite good, especially those from East Germany and Czechoslovakia. But, as a Cuban housewife told me, 'People positively fight each other at the shop counter when Western goods are on sale'.

It is plain that the suppliers from the East cannot really fill the gaps which were left behind when the United States ceased to trade with Cuba. In several industrial establishments I visited it was painfully obvious that production was being severely hampered for lack of spare parts. About one-third of the machinery in the largest cotton works in Cuba—at Bauta, where some 3,500 workers are employed—stood idle. The position was much the same in a leading cigar-making factory in Havana. I saw taxis driving about with their doors fastened on by string.

Castro himself is believed to have voiced privately his disappointment with Russian technical aid and equipment. But he knows that militarily and economically he can survive only if backed by the USSR, for 85 per cent of all goods imported into Cuba now comes from communist countries, 60 per cent from Russia alone. One can see the hand of Russia even behind some of the more magnanimous commitments of eastern Europe in Cuba. In a new trade agreement for the 1965–70 period Bulgaria has agreed to supply Cuba with tractors, television sets, electric motors and other goods on apparently generous credit terms. It is significant, however, that a Soviet-Bulgarian agreement signed in February 1964 specified that 'both governments reaffirm their determination to continue to give full assistance to the glorious Cuban people'. Under this agreement Bulgaria received a loan of 465 million roubles—about £186 million.

No other communist country which I have recently visited, with the possible exception of Bulgaria, seemed to me to be more of a Soviet satellite than Cuba. Newspapers and periodicals gave prominence to items distributed by Soviet agencies. The Soviet news agency, *Novosty*, broadcast its material directly in Spanish over the Cuban radio. New Cuban textbooks, particularly those on economic and political subjects, were almost entirely translations from Russian works. Many of the leading Cuban officials had been trained in the USSR and some 600 Cubans were believed to have been studying at Soviet universities and other educational establishments in 1965.

The Russians seem to be more generous with Cuba than are other communist countries. The Russian arms are apparently provided free of charge, while other eastern Europeans, notably the Czechs, demand payment for military equipment. This only demonstrates that it is Russia rather than her satellites which has the paramount interest in keeping alive the first communist experiment in the tropics.

Outwardly, Cuba's relations with other communist countries are harmonious and inspired by 'socialist brotherhood'. Yet under the surface there are strife and rivalry. 'Our relations with all socialist countries are good,' said Señor Blas Roca, a member of the six-man national executive of the United Party of Socialist Revolution. 'But,' he added, 'our relations with the Soviet Union are especially good'. I talked to him in his office (he was then editor of the chief communist paper, *Hoy*) which was dominated by a huge portrait of Lenin. Blas Roca is a communist of long standing and reputed to be Moscow's strong man in Havana. Any attempt to dislodge him from his positions of influence would surely be interpreted by Moscow as an unfriendly act.

But there are many in the Party who disagree with Russian policies. Some, especially the younger and more militant element, are said to be favouring China. 'You would be surprised,' a Cuban official said to me privately, 'if you knew how much friction there really is between us and the Russians.' Negotiations between Russia and Cuba on any particular subject, especially in economic affairs, are usually prolonged and are marked by heated arguments. I was left in no doubt by Cubans close to government circles that the rocket affair of 1962, when Cuba was virtually left in the lurch by Khrushchev, still rankled.

'But for the Russians, there would be no communism here,' said a Cuban. 'That's the main reason why people don't like them.' The Czechs, Hungarians and other eastern Europeans I saw in Cuba seemed anxious to dissociate themselves from the stigma attaching to the Russians. Yet there was little working in common or association among members of individual eastern European nations. By and large, the eastern Europeans seem to be happy in Cuba. Some have been in the country for two years or more, with their wives and children. Their standard of living on the island is usually a good deal higher than at home.

'I am happy here. I have no desire ever to go back to Prague,' a Czech textile expert told me as we talked in his comfortable flat in the luxury residential hotel, the Sierra Maestra, in Havana. He, his wife and two teenage daughters occupied five large rooms with kitchen and two bathrooms, rent free. There was a private beach attached to the hotel. About four-fifths of the residents were Soviet citizens with their families; the rest were from eastern Europe.

In the hall, propaganda pictures of the Soviet way of life, with flamboyant, triumphant soldiers or happily smiling, un-sophisticated industrial workers or farm boys and girls, dominated the walls. There was also an invitation to a party given by the Hungarians and addressed to members of 'brotherly socialist nations'. But the Czech scientist told me, 'We don't mix much. Each national group sticks to its own.'

Jokes at the expense of the Russians, familiar to all travellers in eastern Europe, now circulate in Cuba. Anti-communist Cubans, especially students and other young people, often make friends with individual east Europeans who happen to share their views, and a surprisingly large number of anti-communist books are available through clandestine channels. I was told that Milovan Djilas's *The New Class*, in Spanish translation, was circulating widely among Cubans and their eastern guests. 'Life here', a Cuban friend said to me, 'is exactly as described by Djilas in his book.'

One could see no evidence that the Soviet bloc countries were following a concerted plan in their operations in Cuba. Rather it seemed that each individual nation was anxious to impress the Cubans with its own particular achievements. The Czechs seemed to be more active than other eastern Europeans in trade and otherwise. They also operate the only commercial passenger airline linking Cuba with the Soviet bloc. Indeed, apart from Madrid, Prague is the only European capital directly connecting with Havana for regular, commercial passenger traffic.

* * *

The Chinese play a subordinate part as Cuba's trading partners, and there is little outward evidence of their presence in the island. For example, one saw no evidence of any Peking activity among the sizeable community of the Cuban Chinese. But it was equally clear that the Chinese were working hard to impress the Cubans with a favourable picture of themselves. Much to the annoyance of Castro himself, the Chinese Embassy in Havana continued to distribute information sheets to Cuban intellectuals and other selected people. Their industrial products as shown in shop windows seemed of unexpectedly high quality, e.g. cotton shirts. Above all, the Chinese seemed anxious to convey the impression of being genuinely sympathetic to the Cubans in their plight.

A Cuban non-communist summed up for me his impressions of the Chinese: 'We like them better because they appear to be more modest than the Russians. They are ready to listen to us and not just to lecture and preach sermons to us.'

But the Russians are clearly determined to stamp out any decisive Chinese influence in Cuba and Castro is far too dependent on the Soviet Union to resist Russian pressure when it affects such a vital matter.

The Russians and other communist foreigners in Cuba do not appear to be directly in charge of any department of industrial enterprise in which they work. But their word carries a good deal of weight. An eastern European technician told me that when he had disagreements with a Cuban he had no difficulty in having him removed from the department to which he was attached.

Yet friction and disagreements are frequent between the Cubans and their sponsors from the East. 'They would not learn from our mistakes,' a Hungarian scientist complained to me about the Cuban economic leaders.

The Cuban communists look with utmost suspicion on any kind of 'revisionism' in international relations as well as in economic life. This explains why Yugoslavia, with her 'special relationship' with the USA and her economic experiments, is the least popular of all communist countries among the Cuban leaders.

'We are creating a new man in Cuba,' Señor Blas Roca explained to me. 'A man who will work for his country and his class rather than just for himself.' Exhortations and slogans which have been discarded in other communist countries in favour of more material incentives are much in evidence in Cuba.

'I am a revolutionary,' the manager of one of the largest industrial enterprises in Cuba—a man in his twenties—said to me. 'I don't work for money.' He told me he was paid a fixed salary of just over £71 a month. The salary for this post had not been changed since 1959. At another factory the manager gave exactly the same figure as his salary. In a tobacco factory in Havana the secretary of the trade union organisation in the enterprise said to me that the workers 'gladly' accepted the wages as fixed by the State.

I found no evidence in Cuban industries of any profit-sharing or incentive pay schemes. There was, however, the institution of *vanguardias*, who constituted some 3 or 5 per cent of the employees in any establishment. These were model workers entitled to special privileges on account of their political awareness or eagerness to do voluntary work. The *vanguardias* might enjoy paid holidays in some favoured resort and in exceptional cases be given free trips to eastern Europe. Of considerable practical value to them is that they are given preference in the distribution of scarce goods. While I was in Havana several thousands of such model workers could be seen queueing for about 500 refrigerators recently supplied by Czechoslovakia. Some of the men and women in the queue had spent nights waiting and were equipped with blankets and flasks.

While some of the Cuban communists no doubt sincerely believe in the possibility of changing human nature I heard others say that it was merely a matter of practical consideration why the Cuban economy must be run from one centre. 'We simply have not enough capable and trustworthy men to allow greater local initiative and independence,' a senior Cuban official told me. 'We are where Russia was during and immediately after the civil war—in the stage of war communism.'

I could see for myself that there must be a good deal of truth in this. I frequently met in Cuba men in positions of responsibility who were extremely young and clearly inexperienced, or men of the *ancien régime* who had little love for, or understanding of, the new state of affairs. Many of them seem to go on hoping that all this will somehow change and disappear, and the old civilisation will come back.

However that may be, a combination of factors makes life particularly difficult in Cuba. This is not to say that life under Castro is necessarily bad in every respect compared with conditions in European communist countries. In many ways standards in Cuba are higher than in Russia. I saw some fairly bad slums in Havana, and housing shortages are acute as new housing is not even keeping pace with the increase in population. But I saw much worse slums in Russia.

The countryside too, and the standards to which the farming population in Cuba seemed to be accustomed in housing and otherwise, were superior to those in the Soviet Union and one or two other communist countries in Europe.

There is certainly more artistic freedom in Cuba than in Russia. It is a well-known fact that some of the leading Cuban communists have been appalled by what they saw of the life in the USSR during their visits. Yet this only accentuates the plight in which Cuba has landed herself. The gap between expectations and the reality of everyday life could not have been wider in any European communist country.

CONCLUSION

THE MAIN conclusion one can draw from looking at life in communist countries is that the revolutions have brought little if any improvement for most of the people. I have not the slightest doubt that even in the Soviet Union, which has propelled herself by communist methods into second place as a world industrial power, wide sections of the population live much worse than people used to live in Russia in 1913, in terms of food, clothing and housing. Most of the elderly people I talked to in Russia, especially in villages, thought they lived considerably better under the Czar.

It is even possible to conclude from Soviet statistics themselves that the real wages of an average industrial worker in Russia were barely higher in 1964 than in the last year of peace under the Romanov dynasty. This does not take into account either the perennial shortages of goods in State shops and the need to purchase food at high, free-market prices, or the very marked deterioration in quality of consumer goods in comparison to pre-Revolution times.

This is not to say that the results of the violent changes carried out by the communists have all been negative or useless. Vast education programmes, one-sided and wasteful though they have been, have none the less represented substantial net gains for the populations concerned, especially in countries where illiteracy was high in the past. Far-reaching industrialisation schemes have diversified and enriched life by providing fresh and varied employment opportunities.

I am not arguing in favour of a return to the régimes or ways of life which existed before communist revolutions. More often than not, communism grew on the shortcomings and frustrations of the old order. Few people I met on my travels in the communist world thought they would wish to live as they did, or their parents did, before the advent of communist régimes.

Change and industrialisation would have been imperative in any case owing to the very high increases of population, especially as emigration opportunities have been much curtailed in recent decades.

But it is in the way the changes have been effected that communism is open to serious criticism.

The weakness of the communist way of economic development is twofold, broadly speaking. First, the communists have failed to solve their farming problems. And industrialisation programmes have failed to take into account a rational usage of available resources and have led to serious dislocations and muddle. Hence the low standard of living in all communist countries. The sorry state of communist agriculture seems to be a particularly important failing and I have felt I should give as much space as possible in this short book to descriptions of various farming systems in communist countries.

The importance of farming cannot be exaggerated. Most of the communist countries were largely rural before their revolutions, although some, including Russia, already had significant beginnings of industrialisation. Most of the people in these countries were peasants in the past—and to a very large extent still live by agriculture.

It is important to recall that, in contrast to developments in communist countries, capitalist industrial revolutions in the West, notably in nineteenth-century Britain, were preceded by a notable expansion of farm output, based on better farming methods. Rapidly rising living standards in Western countries are still very largely based on the growth of the manufacturing industries and of agriculture. So in Britain now, for example, an insignificant proportion of the total labour force produces sufficient food to feed more than half the population. Moreover, such countries as Austria and Denmark (which seem more relevant as examples to eastern Europe) have achieved very high yields even on quite small holdings where these were helped by co-operative movements and sympathetic governments.

The slow progress of farming in communist countries means that large numbers of people must be employed in producing food who could otherwise be working elsewhere. To the already very significant number of people who permanently work in farming—in the Soviet Union these account for one-third of the population, according to official statistics, and to two-fifths according to independent observers—must be added armies of 'volunteers' who include students and members of the armed forces at harvest and other peak periods of farm work, in most communist countries.

Moreover, people in urban employment cannot be adequately fed, and their capacity and will to work are consequently impaired, when the productivity of agriculture is low. Finally, the bill for imports of farm produce represents a heavy burden on the balance of payments in most communist countries.

Industrialisation programmes carried out by accepted communist methods also show very serious flaws. The idea of building heavy industry first, as a base, and then proceeding to change the emphasis in favour of industries benefitting the consumer, has in practice been very difficult to apply. Many communist countries have been saddled with uneconomic projects of steel-making and engineering industries, necessitating large outlays in national resources in order to be kept in operation.

President Tito's cry, 'we have had too many political factories', is now echoed in many other communist countries. Yet the building of grandiose projects seems to be an inherent characteristic of communist régimes, which is very difficult to change. Besides, State-owned businesses, even when self-governing, lack flexibility when it comes to the problem of how to meet the demand of the consumers.

Much of this is now openly admitted in the European communist world. But it still remains to be seen how a communist economy can be successfully reformed. Besides, when proposals and reforms really go far towards achieving a marriage between capitalism and communism the question may legitimately be raised why one should have a communist system in the first place, instead of leaving the economy, or a large part of it, to private enterprise. Such questions are raised by many communists who are baffled by the current wave of 'economic revisionism'.

To those who consider adopting communism as a way of wresting their country from poverty, Cuba offers significant lessons. It has been argued that Cuba represents an extreme case on account of implacable American hostility to a communist régime on its very doorstep. Also there are the exceptional extremism and adherence to 'pure communism' of the Havana leaders. Yet one may also take the view that such a situation is typical rather than exceptional, considering the present context of world tension and the much greater awareness of communist intentions, both on the part of the outside non-communist powers and local populations. If the Cuban communists are labouring under difficult conditions, which in turn partly explains their extremism, this may well be the future case anywhere, especially in Latin America, communism makes new territorial headway.

Communism, although in itself a philosophy of economic progress, is, of course, much more than that. Anyone who has watched the progress of a Communist Party to the position of unchallenged power in a particular country will agree that the motives inspiring those who work for communism are often anything but economic. Frequently a sense of belonging, and comradeship, felt by those who have been participating in the communist movement, are important considerations. Then there are always many power-hungry young men who will welcome a system which offers a unique opportunity to command other people and push them around.

Yet the failure of communist régimes to 'deliver the goods' will be a very serious blow to the future of Marxism-Leninism. As a leading authority in the communist world, the late Soviet Academician Arzumanyan, wrote in 1964: 'If socialism is not production for the sake of consumption by the popular masses, what is the purpose of socialist production?'*

* Quoted from Harry Schwartz, *The Soviet Economy Since Stalin* (Victor Gollancz, London, 1965), p. 241.